T0004912

The
Tending
Years

The
Tending
Years

Understanding Your Child's
Earliest Rituals

J. L. Shattuck

Skinner House Books

BOSTON

www.skinnerhouse.org

Printed in the United States

Cover design by Eric C. Wilder
Cover photo by Getty Images
Author photo by Samantha Myers
Text design by Jeff Miller

print ISBN: 978-1-55896-906-3
eBook ISBN: 978-1-55896-907-0

6 5 4 3 2 1
28 27 26 25 24 23

Library of Congress Cataloging-in-Publication Data

Names: Shattuck, Jennifer L., author.
Title: The tending years : understanding your child's earliest rituals /
    J. L. Shattuck.
Description: Boston : Skinner House Books, [2023] | Summary: "Shattuck
    offers parents new frameworks through which to interpret the ritualistic
    behaviors of their toddlers, as well as reflect on their own practices of
    caregiving"-- Provided by publisher.
Identifiers: LCCN 2023002991 (print) | LCCN 2023002992 (ebook) | ISBN
    9781558969063 (paperback) | ISBN 9781558969070 (ebook)
Subjects: LCSH: Parenting. | Parent and child. | Child psychology.
Classification: LCC HQ755.8 .S523 2023 (print) | LCC HQ755.8 (ebook) |
    DDC 649/.1--dc23/eng/20230417
LC record available at https://lccn.loc.gov/2023002991
LC ebook record available at https://lccn.loc.gov/2023002992

Contents

Introduction

Amateurs

During the first years of my daughter's life, I knew only two things for sure: first, that I loved her deeply, and second, that precisely nothing in my extended career as a childcare provider had prepared me for full-time, 24–7 parenthood. When it came to childcare, I was no longer practicing professionally—this was my life now. I was an amateur.

The list of things that surprised me about my new life was long, especially as we exited the blur of infancy and entered the preschool years. Although I had worked almost exclusively with preschoolers for fifteen years and had what felt like a strong grasp on everything from developmental stages to health and safety to social and emotional development, I frequently felt overwhelmed by a mix of emotions I hadn't known to anticipate: exhaustion and awe.

Over and over, I felt them in equal measure, and often in bewildering combination. It seemed that the things that spread me thin—the endless meals and snacks, the naps and baths and bedtimes—were often the very same ones that connected my daughter and me, that gave me a sense of meaning and purpose, and that allowed my wife and me to teach her the values that meant so much to us. I began to wonder: why?

By the time my daughter was four years old, I was working as a religious educator with a particular focus on the spiritual needs of families with very young children, a job that combined my lifelong interest in child development and my deep love of church. I began to notice, both within the congregation I served and out in my part of the world, that it was common for adults who were caring for children between two and five to feel the same complicated mix of emotions I felt. We were, it seemed, all amateurs: passionate about our work as caregivers, frequently overwhelmed by the needs and behaviors of the kids we loved, intermittently dazzled by the miracle of their very existence. Again, I wondered: Could this particular set of emotions come together for a reason? Could it be equipping us to engage with our kids in a new and deeper way?

Through my work over the past few years, I've come to believe that the answer is yes. I believe that the preschool period, with its potential for both high stress and deep connection, is a unique developmental passage designed to transform adults into the spiritual teachers we're made to be and to lay the groundwork for kids' lifelong faith development. I call this period of childrearing the *tending years* because, for me, the word *tend* (meaning "to care for," and deriving from a Latin root meaning "to stretch") succinctly captures the ongoing, emotionally strenuous process by which caretakers, through the day-to-day work of being in relationship with the children we love, are changed into the leaders they so deeply need.

It takes patience and practice, but slowly, thanks to the kids we love, we can move beyond less helpful ways of understanding and being and begin to inter-act with the world (and the kids themselves) in fresh ways. We can be the spiritual teachers they need. In many ways, we already are. This book is here to prove it to you.

Spiritual?

Many of us would hesitate to apply the words *spiritual teacher* to ourselves. For some, the word *spiritual* has connotations that feel uncomfortable. For others, teaching feels like a responsibility too great to add on top of an already overfilled day. Both of these concerns are understandable. But if you're reading this book right now, you're likely interested in learning how to pass down certain values—kindness, justice, fairness, etc.—to a preschooler in your care. Whatever your beliefs or faith background, these values are spiritual because they connect you to something bigger than yourself: the creatures you love, the universe you live in, the ways of being that matter to you, the mystery that some call God. When we commit to acting as a child's guide as they deepen their relationships with those things (something that, as we'll see in a moment, we all do), we are engaged in spiritual teaching whether we know it or not.

Unspoken Commitments

When children enter the world, the adults who will care for them make three unspoken commitments: to nourish them, to delight in them, and to protect them. Considered one way, these commitments are the stuff of everyday life—we fulfill them by doing concrete, ordinary things like providing food; playing, connecting, and exploring; and giving safety and comfort. Considered another way, these commitments are also inherently spiritual. Every time we feed a child, laugh with them, or comfort them, that child receives the sacred knowledge that they are held in the care of a loving community and a loving universe, valued for exactly the person they are.

In babyhood (from birth to approximately age two), just receiving this knowledge seems to be enough. But after this, for many kids, things shift: instead of letting caretakers live out their commitments to nourish, delight, and protect on their own terms, children begin to reinterpret those commitments in their own ways, turning meals, playtimes, or rest times into rituals with an almost religious flavor. Plates and cups, stuffed animals and pillows become ritual objects. Kisses become blessings, and lullabies hymns.

This, I believe, is where the tending years begin: when preschoolers make the unspoken known by asking us to notice and become intentional about the hidden spiritual elements of our most basic daily routines. It's true that the way they ask isn't always pleasant, and also true that responding isn't always easy. A few paragraphs ago, I called being in relationship with preschoolers "emotionally strenuous," but there's another term for it: hard. If you've recently found yourself exasperated by a child who always needs to drink from the green cup at breakfast or always requires exactly eight kisses at bedtime (and melts down if things aren't proceeding exactly as they desire), you're likely in the midst of the tending years. Ditto if you've argued with a kid who wants to cuddle instead of eat or who insists on micromanaging your play.

I believe these kinds of behaviors are called "challenging" for a reason: because they call us to think differently—to reconsider our commitments, to think through our routines from a child's perspective, and to help them enter the lives of the communities that have cared for them in a new and dynamic way. The theologian Karen Armstrong describes the work of the tending years perfectly when she says that to "know, choose, and love other beings in this world, we have to go outside ourselves." To do so feels, at times, impossibly hard. But over time, the act of going outside ourselves will help us grow as caregivers in ways we never imagined.

About Me (and This Book)

Although I became especially interested in writing this book during my daughter's preschool years, it could be argued that the project has been in development much longer than that—almost my entire life. As is true of many autistic people like me, my memories of my own early childhood are extremely vivid and detailed—much more so, experts have told me, than most people's are. By the time I was eight, I had embarked on a private quest to understand and confirm these early memories. Had I really felt and acted the way I remembered doing? Had the intensity of my joy (and often my anger, sadness, and embarrassment) been real, or was I just imagining it? The work of child development researchers like Louise Bates Ames and T. Berry Brazelton, which I found on my parents' bookshelves, helped and consoled me. Their volumes were designed for adults, but I didn't know or care—all I knew was that the information they contained allowed me to understand the inner life of my younger self. A decade or so later, these same books would inspire me to spend my life working with young children. Since then, the work of other educators, including Bev Bos, Tovah P. Klein, and Dr. Evelyn Moore, has helped me immensely as I've continued to strive to be a loving presence in the lives of the children and families I have served.

INTRODUCTION

This book is for you if:

- You want to understand why the preschoolers you love act the way they do,
- You want to be a supportive guide to the young children you know, or
- You want to understand the spiritual roots of your own caregiving in a new way.

It's not a "how-to" book designed to help you add complicated rituals to your day or implement a whole new system of childrearing. Instead, it's a book that hopes to offer you a new framework through which to interpret the things you're probably already doing—the teaching you already provide. Each of the book's nine chapters addresses a key spiritual teaching—what I call a *hidden spiritual practice*—that you're likely passing down over the course of an ordinary day without even being aware of it. It explains how preschool-age children might be inclined to understand and reimagine the elements of your daily routine and helps you maximize the teaching they receive. Key takeaways from each chapter are bolded to allow for easier reading. At the end of each chapter, a series of reflection questions will invite you to consider how the teachings examined here are appearing in your own caregiving.

Despite my decades of interest and experience, I am still not an expert like the people listed above. Still, it's my hope that the ideas presented here will help you feel more confident in your ability to understand and nurture the preschoolers you love. I hope they will inspire you to keep going on hard days and enjoy the wonderful moments as they happen.

Part One

Nourish

Carlos, two, visibly recoils when he sees that his babysitter has cut his sandwich in half. When reminded that peanut butter is his favorite, Carlos bursts into tears and throws the sandwich on the floor, where it's promptly eaten by the dog.

Five-year-old Kai insists on consuming their breakfast in sequence: oatmeal, then applesauce, then yogurt, then milk. Even on the busiest mornings, they will not be dissuaded from performing what their mother secretly refers to as "the ceremony of the oats."

Sam, age four, refuses to eat (and won't let anyone else eat, either) until each member of the household is present at the table. Dare to take a bite before everyone is seated and Sam will shriek and holler and carry on so inconsolably that those who managed to arrive on time usually come to regret it.

Nia, also four, lingers over every pea and noodle, every sip of milk. Though her exhausted family tries to hurry her along, they find it impossible to get her to eat dinner in less than an hour.

Three-year-old Jadyn will drink only from their favorite pink cup. When told the cup is in the dishwasher, they fling themselves to the ground, sobbing as though the world has ended.

Over my more than twenty years of working with young children, first as a classroom teacher, then as a childcare provider, and finally as both a religious educator and a mom, I've presided over thousands of meals with dozens of kids: in homes and in restaurants, in waiting rooms and church social halls and the back seats of cars, on buses and beaches and picnic blankets. During roughly half those meals, some amount of food was consumed. During the other half . . . well. If you've ever shared more than one meal with a preschooler, you know that not all of them result in the kind of nourishment we adults might have in mind. As in the examples above, many of them ended in tears.

Situations like these can leave caregivers feeling frustrated, disappointed, and powerless. We know we are called to feed the children we love and we take this responsibility seriously, doing everything in our power to make sure they receive the nutrition they need to grow and thrive. For some of us, this is a particularly hard and complicated job. Food deserts and tight grocery budgets may restrict our ability to provide the food we would like to provide in the amounts we would wish. Medical or developmental concerns may make it more difficult for a child to absorb nourishment. And even if we don't have economic or medical reasons to feel anxious about providing adequate nutrition, it's likely we still do, and when the kids we love don't eat the way we think they should, we struggle.

I've been there, and if you're reading this, you probably have too. But over the years I've begun to wonder: what if the behavior that so frustrates us at meals could encourage us instead? What if the sometimes-frustrating behaviors of the preschoolers we love could actually help us give them the kind of spiritual teaching that would strengthen their relationships with us, with their communities, and with themselves?

During the tending years, I believe kids seek to connect with us at meals through three hidden spiritual practices—curiosity, companionship, and replenishment—that help us grow into the supportive guides they crave. Because these requests to connect are commonly behavioral and not verbal, they are often difficult for caregivers to recognize and understand, even as we respond to them (and we do respond to them, even if we don't realize it!).

The chapters in this section will introduce you to various aspects of each hidden practice: where it comes from, how the preschoolers you care for might ask you to engage with it, and the ways you are already doing the spiritual teaching they need.

Chapter One

Curiosity

Why?

For a few short months when my daughter was three years old, her breakfast often consisted of one pancake, a few blueberries, a glass of milk . . . and an imaginary spread of food for a half-dozen stuffed animals whose complicated menu requests she expected me to remember and then serve on invisible plates. Another preschooler I know regularly requested a red cup of "milk-water" every morning and refused to eat until he had received it. Yet another started every dinner hour asking for a single apple, out of which they took one solitary bite before tossing it under the table.

If invisible breakfasts, made-up beverages, and flagrant displays of food waste don't make much sense to you, you're not alone. For many caregivers, much of the behavior kids exhibit at meals during the tending years seems to border on the incomprehensible. *Why?* we ask, groaning internally at what we perceive to be another nonsensical demand. It's a rhetorical question, an understandable expression of our own confusion, frustration, or exhaustion. But it's also something else: a beginning. It's here, with this question, that I believe our development as spiritual teachers begins . . . and we start to ask it much earlier than we realize.

Mutual Wondering

Not all caregivers will have known the children they're caring for since birth, but many of us will have had the experience of spending time with an infant. In addition to being cuddly bundles of delight, they sometimes grimace, root, fuss, or cry, engaging in behaviors known as *care-seeking*. What do these behaviors mean? We don't always know. Faced with a baby in distress, we begin to feel a small flicker of curiosity. *Are they hungry? Are they tired? How can I help?* For many of us, this internal questioning—technically called *empathic concern*—happens so quickly that we don't realize it's happening at all. Invisibly, the willingness to wonder about the inner life of another, and how we can figure out what they need, fuels our ability to connect with them in many ways, including by feeding them.

This hidden practice of curiosity permeates many of a child's first experiences, especially those related to eating. **Spiritually, we could understand their first meals as acts of mutual wondering and exploration— conversations in which both parties come with questions that fuel connection and draw baby and adult together.** Over time, as infants and caregivers meet again and again to ask and answer, trust builds between them. Together, they invent a highly choreographed ritual with its own sacred structure. This ritual contains three phases or sets of questions that I believe affect a child's behavior at mealtime for years to come.

Mealtime: A Curiosity Ritual

PHASE 1: REUNION

The connection questions: "Will you care for me?" / "Is this what you need?"

In the reunion phase of the meal, infant and caregiver come together, often after a period of separation (such as for sleep), to become reacquainted. This phase will often begin with care-seeking. Through rooting, fussing, and other, often quite subtle, expressions of need, a baby will ask their caregiver whether they're able to provide the nurturing they require: "Will you care for me?" In return, hoping they have read the baby's cues correctly, a caregiver responds experimentally by offering food: "Is this what you need?" Where these questions meet for the first time, a relationship is born; as they are repeated again and again over time, they strengthen it.

PHASE 2: ENGAGEMENT
The exploration questions: "Who are you?" /
"How are you doing?"

During the engagement phase of the mealtime ritual, baby and caregiver interact, exploring and mirroring each other. **Meals are social experiences that involve many different sorts of contact: we may gaze at each other, smile, stroke each other's skin, vocalize, or otherwise explore each other at close range.** During this middle phase of a meal, babies may use these gestures as a way of getting to know us, of asking who and how we are, learning how we feel and smell, learning us as a safe place to return to.

For adults, this phase involves not only getting to know the baby they care for but also learning to gauge whether that baby is getting what they need. Is the baby's body relaxing? Do they seem happy and satisfied? This subtle, instinctive paying of attention, called *attunement*, won't ever disappear and will serve caregivers well as children grow.

PHASE 3: CONTENTMENT
*The transition questions: "Can I relax?" /
"What's next?"*

In child development literature, the act of feeding a
baby is what's known as a *biobehavioral regulatory
interaction*—an interaction that helps the minds and
bodies and spirits of both participants become calm.
As the baby eats, both infant and caregiver will feel
their muscles loosen, their breathing slow. The exact
hormonal mechanisms that cause this reaction to
occur are still being explored, but research by Kathryn
Wouk and others tells us that by the end of a meal, it's
common for both baby and adult to feel suffused with
a feeling of well-being and peace.

**Spiritually, the contentment phase of a meal is
a time for affirmation and refreshment.** It's also a
moment of stillness, a transition between this event
and the next. For infants, it's a time to be at ease, totally
relaxed within their relationship with us. For many
caregivers, it's a time when our minds wander to the
future. This is the time we find ourselves planning and

daydreaming, asking questions and preparing ourselves for what's to come. Although we may not realize it yet, this inner curiosity will serve us well in the tumultuous preschool years.

Safekeeping

Through the three pairs of questions that make up the mealtime curiosity ritual, children learn from the adults who love them that eating together is an act of intimacy. To be fed, we show them, isn't just to receive the nutrition they need to survive; it's to be enveloped again and again in a moment of what the writer Elizabeth Gilbert, in her book *Eat, Pray, Love*, calls "ritual safekeeping." Day by day—held and beheld, recognized and remembered with cooing fanfare every few hours by people who love them dearly—children learn to associate eating with feelings of closeness and reassurance.

Years after learning this ritual from the adults who care for them, I believe many preschoolers will continue to try to enact it whenever they eat. The question is: Are we up for the challenge?

Stretching

Though their first meals were only brief interactions that occurred between long intervals of sleep, I believe that preschoolers remember them, although usually not consciously. Moreover, I believe that **many preschoolers spend their mealtimes showing caregivers that they would like to practice that mealtime curiosity ritual with us.** Unfortunately, we ourselves may not remember it. This makes it hard to recognize what's really happening between us and them at meals, even as we respond intuitively to their new questions and move through the phases of the mealtime ritual they are slowly reinventing. We may still feel overwhelmed or frustrated by the behaviors they exhibit. We may wonder whether something is wrong. But could it be that there's good news here?

I believe the frustration and overwhelm we sometimes feel at meals is not only normal, but constructive—part of the mental, emotional, and spiritual stretching workout the kids we love encourage us to undertake during the tending years. Meals are one of the first places this stretching happens. Over the course of months and years, as preschoolers refresh the curiosity ritual that allows them to receive the teaching they crave, they give us the opportunity to wake up to the ways in which our everyday interactions, including eating, influence them spiritually.

Mealtime: A New Curiosity Ritual

PHASE 1: REUNION

The new connection questions: "Am I welcome here?" / "What's really happening here?"

It's common for preschoolers to begin meals with care-seeking behaviors in much the same way that they once did as infants. This care-seeking can take many forms: a child may invite a caregiver to play or imagine, may make demands ("I want the *red* cup!"), or may show sadness or anger (by pushing food away, etc.). Though this behavior looks substantially different from the rooting and fussing that infants do, it indicates a similar need and asks a similar question: "Am I welcome here? Is everything okay?"

Through care-seeking behavior, many preschoolers often ask for indications of consistency at meals— the same cup, the same food, etc.—as evidence that we're ready to receive them. If they don't find the markers of consistency that they expect (because the red cup is in the dishwasher, or because we ran out of the cereal they like), they may begin to feel anxious and distressed. Maybe, they think, they're *not* welcome. What now?

To understand how this works, imagine yourself at your favorite neighborhood restaurant. You arrive, get seated, greet the friends you've met for dinner, chat a little about work and the weather. Everything is proceeding beautifully until you go to order and realize no one has a menu. For a moment, things feel slightly off-balance. A tiny, anxious segment of your brain begins to wonder, almost imperceptibly, if something is wrong. Did the staff somehow forget about you? Is the kitchen closed? *What now?*

So it is for preschoolers whose care-seeking goes unrecognized. During the reunion phase of the mealtime ritual, their care-seeking behavior asks for confirmation that we recognize, remember, and love them. When caregivers incorrectly interpret care-seeking as misbehavior, meals can become stressful.

No matter how we interpret care-seeking at the start of meals, we still respond with an intuitive curiosity: *What's going on here? Why is this happening?* As was mentioned at the beginning of the chapter, sometimes this question is an expression of something other than compassion. Still, even if we're asking it out of frustration and overwhelm, I believe the question is evidence that we're acting in our capacity as spiritual teachers, engaging with the children we love in the practice of mutual wondering.

PHASE 2: ENGAGEMENT
The new exploration questions: "What are we doing?" / "Who are you becoming?"

For preschoolers, meals are a site of what psychologists call *vicarious learning*, or learning through observation.

15

Through the act of eating with caregivers, preschoolers gain a vast amount of knowledge about everything from the foods that are eaten in their culture to the values that are important in their communities.

Vicarious learning at meals looks like much more than just sitting and watching. (If you spend a lot of time with preschoolers, you know that it almost *never* looks like just sitting and watching!) As we'll discuss in the next chapter, a child may engage in multiple forms of investigation that help them understand how meals work. They may play with food, exploring textures and flavors that are unfamiliar to them. They may ask to sit in a caretaker's lap or to eat from their dish. Through these behaviors, I believe children encourage us, their caregivers, to model the things they need to know.

In response to this encouragement, caregivers engage with a preschooler much as we do with infants, instinctively attuning to a child's body language or behavior in ways that allow us to receive more information about the children we're caring for than we might be consciously aware of. We absorb everything from their mood to how much food they consume to the new things they're learning, and subconsciously adjust our teaching to meet their needs.

PHASE 3: TRANSITION
The new reassurance questions: "What's next?"/ "Can I relax now?"

In infancy, the mealtime curiosity ritual often ends with a calm, peaceful adult and a tranquil (maybe even sleeping) baby. In the tending years, the contentment phase can look profoundly different. As we'll explore in-depth during the third chapter of this section, a pre-schooler who feels affirmed and full is likely to feel energized and ready to move on to the next activity. By contrast, caregivers often crave a break. In the transition phase, many of us ask ourselves what we'll need to make it through the rest of the day. A cup of coffee? A few moments of downtime? Showing this curiosity about our own needs—even if we can't meet them immediately—is part of our spiritual development as caregivers and can help us model for the children we love how to take care of ourselves during stressful moments.

THE WAY TO CURIOSITY

Two Ways You Might Already Be Engaged in This Spiritual Practice

Even if the mealtime rituals outlined here have been invisible to you until now, you've still been engaging with the practice of curiosity! Here are two ways in which your instinctive, natural inquisitiveness has been helping you nurture the preschoolers you care for.

1. Noticing patterns

As you interact with the child you care for at meals, your natural ability to attune to them has been allowing you to notice patterns and wonder about them. For instance, you might notice times when the child is apt to feel hungry or when they're more likely to engage in care-seeking. We're often unaware that we're doing this, even as we subtly adjust our teaching to reflect what we've learned about a child's needs.

In addition to noticing patterns related to the kids we love, we can also notice patterns about our own development as spiritual teachers. Where are we consistently being stretched? What lessons keep appearing to us again and again? How are we responding to them?

2. Asking with compassion

Preschoolers aren't the only ones who benefit from the practice of curiosity—caregivers do as well! As we've seen, eating with preschoolers can be tough. Inevitably, there are days when we will struggle. But there are also days when, even in the midst of the struggle, we recognize that we're doing our best. When we take the time to pause and show gentle curiosity about why certain feelings are surfacing in us (*Why do I feel so annoyed about this? Where is this feeling coming from?*), the same way we would with the kids we love, we allow ourselves time to respond instead of react— something that can help us be more present overall.

Coming Up Next

In the next two chapters, we'll be exploring how the last two elements of the mealtime ritual—*engagement* and *transition*—open us to new and different spiritual practices. Before you continue, please take a moment to answer the reflection questions below in whatever way works for you: mentally, in conversation with friends or loved ones, or on paper.

Reflection Questions

1. In what ways do you notice the preschoolers you care for engaging in care-seeking behavior at the start of meals? How do you notice yourself reacting to it?

2. How has the behavior of the preschoolers you care for allowed you to get to know them better? Have you noticed yourself adjusting your teaching in response to this behavior?

3. If you haven't already, experiment with asking yourself about your needs during the transition phase of the meal ritual. What would relaxation look like for you?

Chapter Two

Companionship

Togetherness

For many preschoolers, the perfect dining partner has three characteristics: an empty lap, a full plate, and a patient soul. Though the act of eating may seem ordinary to adults, to young kids it's endlessly fascinating—and many of them want a front-row seat every time we do it. If you've ever eaten with a child who was inclined to clamber up into your chair, pluck the choicest morsels from your bowl while ignoring their own food, eat while clinging to your neck, or run around while eating, you may have wondered (perhaps with some exasperation) what it is about preschoolers that makes so many of them want to consume their food this way.

These behaviors too have their roots in the first days and weeks of life, and although they might seem disruptive or rude, they can create an ideal environment in which to receive spiritual teaching. Just as they did when they were babies, preschoolers act in ways that enable a sense of togetherness and help us make meals a community event that nourishes much more than hungry bellies. The difficulty is that they may disagree with us about what sort of guidance we should offer.

Under Pressure

During the preschool years, it becomes clear that many kids and caregivers have different opinions about what meals are for. Studies of adults caring for preschoolers during mealtime (including one with the highly relatable title "Just Three More Bites") have shown that the primary mealtime objective of most caregivers is to get children to eat. Studies of preschoolers, on the other hand, show that they tend to view meals differently. **For them, meals are not about food.** Despite what their caregivers might prefer (and despite all our attempts to get them to do otherwise), young children spend much of their time at meals not eating the way we wish they would, but instead trying to maintain their physical and emotional connections to us. In many cases, they try to strengthen community bonds by creating what researcher Katherine Chandler, in a study on children's behavior at meals, calls "playful and humorous experiences" while eating—in other words, doing things that drive adults bananas.

For many caregivers, this "playful and humorous" behavior (and the underlying disagreement over what a meal is for) can make eating with preschoolers something to dread. Understandably frustrated that our nutritional goals for the kids we love are likely to be thwarted by their own silliness, we sometimes seek to take control of the situation and make mealtime run to plan by resorting to what are called *pressure tactics*. Pressure tactics can include extolling the virtues of certain foods ("these carrots will make you big and strong!"), monitoring consumption ("just three more bites!"), or incentivizing with treats ("eat your beans and you can have dessert!"). While these efforts may work in the short term, many kids push back eventually. In response to feeling pressured, they'll often ramp up the silliness—not to misbehave, but in an attempt to get us to drop the pressure and connect more fully with them. **For preschoolers, meals are about full engagement.** Just as when they were infants using their newly developing social skills (smiling, vocalizing, etc.) to engage with caregivers one-on-one and skin-to-skin, many will use mealtimes to ask that we take on a new teaching role: that of *companion*.

Companions

Though it now has the more general meaning of "friend" or "partner," the word *companion* once referred specifically to a person with whom food was consumed.

(*Companionem*, the Latin word it descends from, literally means "bread fellow" or "messmate.") **To engage in the hidden spiritual practice of companionship is simply to eat with the kids we love while prioritizing closeness over consumption and community over conflict.** Preschoolers will use a number of connective strategies that involve nestling close to a caregiver while eating, unsubtly showing us that closeness is their top priority at meals, and this reminder can inspire us to become the companions they need.

To remember these strategies and their role in creating closeness between children and caregivers, I use the acronym SPOON, which stands for *shared consumption, physical connection, offerings, observation,* and *novelty.* These strategies can sometimes leave caregivers feeling irritated or overwhelmed. But they can also remind us to understand meals differently—and to understand ourselves as the spiritual teachers we were made to be. To appreciate how they work to facilitate closeness at meals, let's examine them one at a time.

Shared consumption

At some point during any given meal, many kids are likely to leave their own food behind and express a desire to eat from a caregiver's dish instead. Why? Research from the social sciences can help us make some sense of this. Kaitlin Woolley and Ayelet Fishbach, in two studies aptly titled "A Recipe for Friendship" and "Shared Plates, Shared Minds," respectively, found that when members of a community engage in what's known as *shared consumption* (eating the same food from the same dish, a common practice in many cultures), they're likely to feel higher levels of cooperation and to experience lower levels of conflict—things that one imagines might be useful in a community that involves preschoolers! Other studies, like a 1998 one from the *Journal of Nutrition*, have found that children eating from the same dish as a loved one are more likely to try unfamiliar foods, to focus their attention on eating for a longer period of time, and to be more receptive to teaching.

For preschoolers, people who eat the same food they are eating become family. The kids we love often choose to eat from our laps and bowls not because the food we serve them separately isn't appealing (it is often the same food, after all), but because the food we serve them separately doesn't foster closeness or strengthen community bonds the same way food from a shared dish does. As with every other aspect of the meal, preschoolers prefer food to serve their vision of what a meal should be. The takeaway? When we share food and eat together, we grow together.

Physical connection

Many a caregiver has had to learn to eat with a preschooler curled in their lap, perched on their hip, or holding their hair. The good news? Humans are far from alone in this predicament. In many primate species, juvenile members of the community regularly engage in what's known as *cofeeding*, or eating while attached to an adult caregiver. Among chimpanzees, some of our closest primate cousins, young will nurse until around age five, continuing to get at least some of their nutrition while clinging to their caregiver's body even as they learn to forage on their own.

For human kids, eating while physically connected to a trusted adult provides several of the same benefits that cofeeding does for juvenile chimps. First, because it's reminiscent of the first meals they ate as newborns, meals consumed this way may be particularly comforting and peaceful. Second, eating while connected provides an efficient way for us to model what it means to eat in our communities—everything from our traditional foods to the utensils we use to eat it to the manners that our culture considers socially acceptable. Observing these things at close range helps kids absorb the teachings of their communities in an intuitive, efficient way.

Offerings

One way that preschoolers may choose to foster closeness with caregivers at meals is through the bringing of offerings—objects that allow child and caregiver to connect around something other than food. An offering may take the form of a beloved stuffed animal or book, a leaf found on the sidewalk, or anything at all that a child finds interesting.

The philosopher David Hawkins, who spent the latter part of his career studying early childhood education, explained in his essay "I, Thou, and It" how offerings promote feelings of closeness between adults and young children. "One of the very important factors in [meeting and talking with children]," he wrote, "is that there be some third thing which is of interest to the child and to the adult." His wife, the writer and educator Frances Hawkins, expanded on this idea when she said, in a short essay on her own website, that "in sharing enjoyment with a child there is a communication of the fact that as observers and learners we are of the same stuff." When children bring offerings—what David Hawkins calls "third things"—to meals, they invite us to spend time on their level, as something close to intellectual and spiritual equals.

Observation

As we learned in the last chapter, in their early years children learn a great deal through watching the people with whom they are in close relationships—caregivers, siblings, friends, etc.—and then imitating their behavior. At meals, learning through observation might look like playing with food, blowing bubbles in a beverage, attempting to join in conversation by screeching or yelling, or any number of other behaviors that, depending on our culture or life experiences, we might be inclined to view as rude or disruptive.

Psychologist Alfred Bandura, who originated the theory of vicarious learning, used the term *apprentice* to describe people who are learning vicariously. I believe this word can help us reframe these sorts of behaviors and remember where they come from: beginners who are trying their best. As companions, we are called to guide and accompany these beginners as they learn what it means to be in community with others. One way to do this is to ignore the behaviors that annoy us and keep modeling the ones we'd like to encourage. Over time (although it may take a while), kids will learn by watching!

Novelty

During the preschool years, kids are learning and growing at an intense rate. As they did when they were infants, many of them will use the things they're learning to capture our attention and invite us to engage with them in ways that foster closeness. Mealtime research on preschoolers by Katherine Chandler has found that these invitations often appear as wordplay and general silliness: "By playing with words and rhyming within the process of eating and passing the food around the table . . . children engaged in humorous routines repetitively." Meal after meal, kids will find new, engaging ways to capture our attention—and keep repeating them until it's clear they have done so.

Other invitations to engage might look like singing, dancing, or eating food in a silly way. When we

welcome these behaviors knowing what they mean—
that the kids we care for are excited to be with us—it
makes it easier to respond to them playfully.

THE WAY TO COMPANIONSHIP

Three Ways You Might Already Be Engaged in This Spiritual Practice

Behind each SPOON strategy is a request for
deeper connection, cooperation, and teaching.
Through them, the preschoolers we love will
invite us to understand and eat meals the way
they prefer to: connected to us. Some caregivers
will respond intuitively and immediately to these
connective strategies, while others will need to
engage with them over a longer period of time.
Either of these is completely normal! No matter
how you respond, here are three ways you might
already be practicing companionship with the
preschoolers you love.

1. **Eating "family style"**

   Not every caregiver will feel comfortable allowing a child to eat from their lap, but many naturally recreate the closeness fostered by shared consumption through eating "family style," in which each person serves themselves from a common dish or platter. Just as they do when engaging in shared consumption, kids who eat family style learn a variety of positive ways of being, including how to share, to cooperate, and to engage in or attend to mealtime conversations.

2. **Storytelling**

   In his book *The Cooking Gene: A Journey Through African American Culinary History in the Old South*, writer and food historian Michael W. Twitty reminds us that "many of our most pungent memories are carried through food, just as connections to our ancestors are reaffirmed by cooking the dishes handed down to us." All of us have foods that feel profoundly connected to our cultural heritage. When we eat these foods beside the children we love, sharing both flavor and the stories connected to that dish, we offer them a link to the generations that came before. If you are doing this at meals—either intentionally or not—the kids you love gain a stronger connection to the past and to the cultural communities they live in, which may have a profound effect on them as they grow.

3. **Singing and rhyming together**

As we saw earlier in this chapter, many preschoolers are naturally inclined to bond with friends and loved ones through wordplay. Adults often use rhythmic invitations like blessings, table graces, songs, and other ritual elements to begin a meal. When we do this, we signal to the preschoolers we love that we understand their desire for joyful routines at meals and that we're committed to joining them in their joy. If you have been doing this, give yourself a high five!

Coming Up Next

In the next chapter, we'll discover how the last stage of the mealtime ritual, transition, can help us become more compassionate about our own caregiving and our own needs. Before you continue, please take a few moments to answer the reflection questions below in whatever way works for you—and to notice the places you feel yourself growing and developing as a spiritual teacher.

Reflection Questions

1. Do you notice the preschoolers you love using SPOON strategies to connect with you? Which ones do they seem to use most often?

2. Think for a moment about the food you're serving the preschoolers you care for. What stories connect to this food? Have you shared them yet?

3. In what ways do you notice yourself growing to be able to engage more playfully at meals with the children you care for?

Chapter Three

Replenishment

The Circus

The other night, a friend mentioned to me that she and her wife were having trouble managing their two pre-schoolers after dinner. "The minute we try to clean up or get anything done," my friend said, "they get into *everything*. Every night it's pure chaos." I laughed in recognition, remembering the days when I, caring for three children under age four, spent meals thinking that I might finally be on top of things only to realize, the moment I began to wash the dishes, that pande-monium was unfolding in the other room.

If a quick internet search is any indication, my friend and I are not alone here. Facebook parenting groups are full of people wondering why their kids are so hyper after dinner, and to read academic studies of preschoolers and mealtimes is to find caregiver after caregiver describing the aftermath of meals using the word "circus." Clearly, many adults are struggling to cope—and if you're caring for preschoolers, you might be as well. But could the behavior that bothers some of us so much be a sign that we're doing something right? And could it also give us insight into what we ourselves need?

Mealtime Emotional Climate

Think about the last time you shared a meal with loved ones. Who was present? What did you eat? How did you feel?

If eating with friends or family rejuvenated you, you're in good company. **For the preschoolers we love,**

eating with those closest to them often provides a sense of fullness and refreshment that has little to do with the food and drink that was served. Even after a meal has concluded and guests have dispersed, a preschooler may continue to feel energized and light-hearted, buoyed by a sense of well-being and joy. For many, this energy peaks about fifteen to thirty minutes after a meal has ended and might take the form of a pillow fight, wrestling match, or shrieking contest. Despite how we adults might feel about it, this behavior doesn't spring from a desire to make our lives more difficult. It comes from a feeling of *replenishment.*

To be replenished is to be filled up completely—not only with food and drink, the dictionary tells us, but also with that which helps us thrive in other ways. **For preschoolers, meals are the ultimate source of replenishment.** When they gather with us, whether it's in a formal setting or in a casual environment where they're grabbing a quick snack, they look to us to satisfy both their hunger for physical nourishment and their hunger for love and affirmation. When we do satisfy it, we create what's called a positive *mealtime* *emotional climate.* The mealtime emotional climate is simply the quality of emotions expressed by those who are dining together, and a positive one is created whenever people use meals to foster feelings of closeness with one another. As we saw in chapter 2, preschoolers are naturally good at this: they use meals to tell stories or jokes, to share things that are important to them, and to be physically connected with caregivers. When we affirm their inclination toward these things and join them in their efforts, we contribute to a positive emotional environment for eating. The better eating with us feels, the more connected preschoolers feel to us and the better they feel about themselves once the meal has ended.

Replenished

What does this have to do with a preschooler's high energy after meals? A lot, it turns out. **When the kids we love get rambunctious after eating, I believe they're telling us we've done our job in creating a positive mealtime climate. We've fed them, filled**

them up, and let them know how much they matter to us. We've practiced replenishment, they're content, and they're experiencing this contentment with their whole selves—loudly. This is excellent news, except for one thing: *we're tired*. And sometimes we can't help but show it.

If you've gotten cranky with a preschooler who's become boisterous after eating, you're not alone. The downside to a positive mealtime emotional climate—proof that we're nourishing the kids we love in all the ways that matter—is that many kids will spend the post-meal period invigorated to a level that some caregivers find hard to tolerate. **This is one of the hard truths of caregiving: what replenishes the children we love often depletes us.** And is it any wonder that we'd find meals a little draining? After all, we've prepared food and supervised its consumption. We've guided conversations and modeled everything from good manners to cherished values. After all that, we've helped to wipe the messy faces and wash the dishes too. When all is said and done, how many of us would like the kids we love to settle down for a bit?

43

I've been there more days than I can count. But I've also come to believe that the period of excitability that often occurs after meals serves a hidden purpose in our spiritual lives. As with so many of the behaviors preschoolers exhibit during the tending years, I believe their joy and excitement can truly help us grow. How? By inviting our own reactions to it, the preschoolers we love are showing us that we don't have to stay depleted. I think they're encouraging us to ask *how we ourselves might need to be replenished.*

Mind the Gap

At some point during the years I spent caring for extremely young children, I realized that the natural gap between meals and the activities that came next—the transitional period the kids I was caring for used to demonstrate their couch-jumping levels of replenishment—was giving me a moment to reflect on my own needs. At first, the idea of stopping to consider what I myself needed seemed selfish. *There's too much to do,* I told myself. *The kids need me. I'm fine.* But the truth was that my reactions were telling a different story. I wasn't fine—I was struggling. In response to the lively behavior of the kids I cared for (behavior that wasn't in and of itself a problem), I was feeling strong emotions that were giving me valuable information about my unmet spiritual needs and how I might meet them.

Slowly, after making sure that the kids I cared for were safe to play, I began to experiment with taking a short break between lunch and "quiet time" to scribble down, on whatever piece of paper I had handy, my answers to three questions:

- What am I feeling right now?
- What does this feeling mean?
- What does this feeling tell me I need?

It didn't take long—only about five minutes a day—and after trying the practice for a few weeks, I had collected quite a pile of notes. Looking through the mix of junk mail, notepaper, and stray napkins, I found patterns: certain emotions popped up again and again. So did cravings for particular indulgences I associated with rest and time alone. While the answers to these questions will be different for every caregiver, a little research showed me that some of my emotional reactions were common, and they often pointed to particular needs.

Common Emotional Reactions and Their Meanings

Feeling overwhelmed: a need for quiet

It's common for caregivers, particularly those who are introverted, highly sensitive, or neurodivergent, to feel overwhelmed by the rambunctious behavior of the kids they care for. This overwhelm can often be difficult to describe—at my house we still use a phrase originated by my then-four-year-old daughter, "my brain is going emergency," that captures, somewhat imprecisely, the feeling of mental and emotional pressure that accompanies noisy environments. Often, a feeling of overwhelm can signal a need to withdraw—to find for ourselves a bit of quiet.

If you spend your days with preschoolers, you know that if there's one or more in the vicinity, true withdrawal is probably not a possibility. But I found that a little inner quiet—a chance to briefly "sit down on the inside," as the writer Emily P. Freeman puts it in an episode of the podcast *The Next Right Thing*—could be found or cultivated in small moments. For me, the bathroom provided a brief respite from the mayhem—and time to plan to take a real break in a quiet place as soon as the opportunity arose.

Feeling anxiety: a need for grounding

Sometimes, when kids get hyper or rambunctious after a meal, our bodies and minds interpret their raucousness as a sign of danger. This isn't our fault—as human beings, we're just made that way. Like the brains of our earliest ancestors, our own brains are designed to react strongly to noises—the roar of a tiger, the cry of a baby—that signal a possible threat to our safety or the safety of those we love. To help us either conquer or escape from the source of the danger, loud noises trigger the release of adrenaline, the fight-or-flight hormone. While there are times that a surge of adrenaline might be helpful, there are other situations in which it is very much not.

When a surge of adrenaline combines, for instance, with our very real concerns about broken bones or smashed lamps, it may cause us to overreact to the enthusiasm of the kids we care for with snapping, yelling, or other reactions we might not be proud of.

One possible solution to this issue—and something that worked well for me—is to practice grounding or centering techniques. These techniques, which include deep breathing, meditation, tapping, and others, can help us disconnect from our worries and allow us to recognize what's actually happening in the moment: the kids are safe, the kids are happy, and, in just a few minutes, they (and you!) will be ready to move on to whatever comes next.

Feeling anger: a need for rest

Sometimes, even after we've grounded ourselves, we may feel lingering traces of frustration or anger. (I know I did.) Even if we don't express these feelings, we may roil inside with resentment of our interminable to-do list or our poor night's sleep—things that point to our need for a period of recuperation. An exhausted brain is more apt to react negatively to situations that feel beyond our control—including a loud environment.

If you find that you're consistently reacting to the post-lunch energy break with feelings of anger, your body and brain might be craving true rest. Even on days when such a thing seemed impossible, writing down my need helped me figure out when I might be able to fit some rest in.

If you try answering the three questions I offered above, you might notice yourself experiencing other emotions not listed here. The more often you take the time to sit with those feelings, the better you may become at figuring out what they mean for you.

THE WAY TO REPLENISHMENT
Two Ways You Might Already Be Engaged in This Spiritual Practice

During the long, often exhausting days that make up the tending years, those of us who care for young children may struggle to prioritize our own needs. It may be challenging for us to recognize that caring for ourselves (even for short periods of time) is an integral part of our role as spiritual teachers, but I strongly believe it is. **When we model taking care of ourselves, we show the kids we love that it's all right for them to do so as well.** Here are some ways you're likely modeling the practice of replenishment for the kids you love:

1. **Using your words**

   If you're feeling overwhelmed, frustrated, or cranky after meals and you take the time to say so ("I'm feeling overwhelmed by all the noise, so I'm going to sit here on the couch for a minute and calm my body," for example), you're showing the kids you care for that replenishment is a priority. This matters not just because you're modeling good spiritual care, but because you're also helping them find the language they may someday use to express their own needs and to get the help they need to meet them.

2. Taking a break

We know it's not always possible to take a break while caring for the kids we love. But even if we take a break they don't know about—during nap time or after they're asleep for the night—we're still practicing a form of replenishment that benefits both us and them. Rested brains and bodies are flexible brains and bodies—when we prioritize rest, we're better prepared to handle whatever the kids we love throw at us!

Coming Up Next

In the next section of this book, Delight, we'll be discovering the three hidden spiritual practices of play: narration, improvisation, and immersion. Before you move on, please take a moment to consider the questions below.

Reflection Questions

1. Think of meals you've recently eaten with the preschoolers you care for. What words would you use to describe the emotional climate of those meals?

2. In what ways do the kids you care for tend to tell you that they feel replenished after meals . . . or that they need more care and affirmation from you?

3. How have you been practicing replenishment without realizing it? List the ways and then congratulate yourself!

Part Two

Delight

Violet, age two, loves to roughhouse and wrestle. All day long, she tries to engage the people around her in physical play: climbing on them, pulling at their clothes and hair, giggling when they get frustrated. The adults who care for her can't help but wonder if something is wrong. *Isn't this too rough?* they ask each other worriedly. *Should we stop this?*

Three-year-old Mohammed wants people to follow the rules of the game. *His* rules, that is. The problem for his family? Those rules are always changing! They

53

want to play with him, but it's exhausting to try to keep up.

Quinn, age four, loves to organize. Beads, blocks, sequins—anything small gets sorted and placed with others of its kind. Her babysitter, watching, wonders if they should redirect her to an activity that's more fun. After all, shouldn't Quinn want to be *playing*?

Three-year-old Emerson won't take off their super-hero cape. Whether they're having a snack, zooming around the apartment making "brave noises," or taking a nap, the cape is always there. In private, their parents talk: the cape is getting dirty and is starting to need repairs. Should they take it away? And why does Emerson insist on wearing it all day, anyway? Should something be done?

Yesterday at the park, I watched a small child, about two years old, living their best life. In just a few minutes, they engaged in seemingly every form of play known to humankind: they climbed and swung and chased and roared like a tiger. They fashioned tools out of sticks and dug, singing to themselves some half-remembered song. They plunged their hands in the cool sand under the swing set and then flung them in the air, showering other small children with a confetti-like blessing of granules. All around them, a cadre of adults called out warnings to the kids in their care: "Be careful; play nice; no throwing!"

Over the years, I've spent a lot of time as part of this warning crowd. Maybe you have too. Afraid of horseplay because someone might get hurt. Slightly suspicious of noise because what if things get out of control? Keeping watch to ensure that toys are shared. It's understandable that caregivers feel they must be vigilant in play spaces—after all, when you're responsible for small children, you want to do everything you can to make sure they're safe and loving and kind. But even though it's understandable, it presents a problem: when we spend our time fretting, we tend to miss out on the delight the kids we love are experiencing... and they're experiencing a lot of it!

The word *delight* comes from a Latin root meaning "to allure or entice." As human beings, we're inexorably drawn to the new, the interesting, the unique: to touch it, taste it, savor it. The world, with its inviting textures and flavors, calls us to engage, and we do. This engagement is called play, and all of us, no matter how old we are, do it. Preschoolers, of course, do it more than grown people, and to watch them at length is to notice how much a preschooler's play behavior has to tell us about who they are and how they understand the world.

It's become something of a sentimental cliche to talk about children as teachers of adults. But, like many cliches, this one has a kernel of truth at its heart: we do learn so much from being with children and from experiencing the world as they do. During the tending years, the kids we love will invite us to do just that. Through play, they'll model another set of hidden spiritual practices (narration, improvisation, and immersion) that will not only help us delight in being with them but will allow us to introduce them to everything from the concepts of bodily autonomy and consent to the joys of contemplation . . . all in ways that are so instinctive as to be nearly invisible, even to us!

DELIGHT

As in the last section, the next three chapters will introduce you to various aspects of each hidden practice: its roots, the ways in which it often shows up in a preschooler's behavior, and the many ways you are already giving the kids you love the spiritual teaching they need.

Chapter Four

Narration

Too Much?

As a caregiver of preschool-age kids, I've been climbed
like a ladder, ridden like a horse, and chased like a
mouse. If you spend much of your time with young children and you too sometimes feel like a human playground, you're not alone. And if you sometimes worry
about it, wondering if this kind of interaction is too
aggressive, too dangerous, or just plain too much? It
turns out you're in good company there, too. For decades,
those who study the development of preschoolers have

been debating whether what's officially called "rough-and-tumble play" (energetic play that includes physical contact with others and incites feelings of exhilaration and joy) is helpful or harmful to kids. Their questions— *Are these activities safe? Do they help children learn or do they interfere with learning? Should we encourage or limit them?*—are probably familiar to anyone who has ever been responsible for a preschooler's well-being. One thing researchers can agree on is that whether it's helpful or harmful, the majority of kids enjoy some form of rough-and-tumble play . . . and want the adults who love them to enjoy it as well. But why? And where does the urge to engage in it come from?

I believe the answer could be found in the form of a hidden spiritual practice that's tucked inside the sort of rambunctious, high-energy activities that tend to give adults so much anxiety (and children so much happiness!). Even as we feel caught between keeping kids safe and providing opportunities for fun, this practice allows us to continue acting as spiritual teachers, whether we realize we are doing so or not, working with kids from the very start of life to help them understand what it means to relate to others with kindness and compassion.

Love Stories

If you've ever interacted with what Hillary Rodham Clinton, in her book *It Takes a Village*, called "those helpless bundles of power and promise" known as human babies, you know that most adults just can't help it: we find ourselves driven by some inner force to nuzzle, tickle, cuddle, and wiggle them. We may clap their hands, bounce them on our knees, toss them gently in the air, or zoom them around like airplanes. In her book *Joyful*, author Ingrid Fetell Lee writes that this behavior stems from an instinctive psychological reaction known as the *cuteness response*. In the cuteness response, the smiles and joyful burbles of infants encourage adults to respond to, care for, and bond with them in physical ways that promote their well-being—in other words, to play with them. And what does play have to do with well-being? More than we know!

In their book *The Art of Roughhousing*, play researchers Anthony T. DeBenedet, MD, and Lawrence J. Cohen, PhD, suggest that when children engage in this sort of gentle but vigorous interaction with caring adults, they receive a series of unspoken messages that affirm their unique selfhood and provide a sense of belonging. As a religious educator, I believe that these messages are part of the hidden spiritual practice of narration. **When we engage in the practice of narration, our actions tell a series of love stories that the children we care for will carry with them as they grow.** These stories fit into three different, equally sacred categories, each type playing its own role in helping kids and adults connect playfully and learn from each other.

The Sacred Stories of Rough-and-Tumble Play

You are here: a love story about bodies
"Play," say the writers Frederic and Mary Ann Brussat on their website Spirituality and Practice, "is the exuberant expression of our being." When we engage in

rough-and-tumble play with the children we love, we unknowingly communicate a deep gladness in this being. Without even being aware of it, we model our joy in having a body and of having the capacity to engage with other bodies. Even gentle activities like rocking can pass down the spiritual teaching that being here together, self to physical self, is a gift. "You are precious and worthy," our behavior says. "In all that you do and are, you are so loved." For babies, this initial love story is perhaps the one that will stay with them the longest and have the greatest influence on their later behavior: for the next few years, physically connecting with others through play will be the primary way many of them will show interest, love, and affection.

You are fun: a love story about shared joy
Although not all types of play are done in groups, rough-and-tumble interactions require the willing participation of at least one other person to be entertaining. Even in babyhood, the cuteness response ensures that physical play is inherently social and creative. By instinctively welcoming the kids we love into relationship

with us in new, mutually enjoyable ways that shift as they grow (moving from rocking to peekaboo to bouncing and swinging), caregivers model for kids that community is built on experiences of shared cherishing and shared joy. "People who have fun together," our actions say, "are people who love each other." Over time, as the kids we love grow out of babyhood and into the preschool years, this message will inspire kids to use a variety of play behaviors to connect with us and with each other.

You are safe: a love story about boundaries

At some point during any given play session, a baby is likely to decide they've had enough. To communicate their desire to stop engaging in whatever activity they've been participating in, an infant might look away, pull back, or vocalize. When a caregiver is attuned to these signs and ends the interaction accordingly, they send a variety of messages about power and consent. "Your boundaries matter," they say. "I will listen to you. You are safe with me." Spiritually, the gentle rough-and-tumble play of infancy offers a number of opportunities for babies to learn about how to connect with others responsively and respectfully. Later, more intensive forms of rough-and-tumble play will give kids (and adults) endless chances to reinforce gentle lessons about power, bodily autonomy, and emotional boundaries.

Through the love stories of narration, caregivers have the chance to imbue even the silliest activities with deep meaning. But as with the other spiritual practices we're exploring in this book, most of us are unaware of narration's power in the lives of the children we love or even the fact that we're passing down stories at all. As they enter the preschool years, I believe that kids will look to the adults in their lives to continue the teaching we began when they were small, hoping that we will attend to the stories they tell about the world through play. Instinctively, we will—and in the process, we'll be given a new challenge: the chance to think like a preschooler and reconsider some of what we know about rough-and-tumble play. How will we rise to this challenge? By scaffolding.

Scaffolding

During the tending years, caregivers are invited to reconsider all we think we know about the kids we love. Of all the preschool-era behaviors that might stretch caregivers into different ways of thinking and being, rough-and-tumble play is one of the more challenging because it seems to fly in the face of everything we want for the kids we love. How, so many of us wonder, can they grow into the kind, loving people we want them to be when they spend so much of their time playing rough with us and others? Shouldn't we do something?

This is often the issue that makes the tending years so difficult: because we caregivers are adults, we think like adults and view the behavior of the kids we love through an adult lens. Rough-and-tumble play is a common example of this: it's easy for caregivers to consider much of the physical play preferred by the kids we love to be inappropriate or unsafe because it would be in adults. If your coworkers said hello to you each morning the way some preschoolers like to say hello to their friends—by chasing you around the room or by hug-wrestling you down to the floor—you'd likely complain to Human Resources. For preschoolers, this common way of greeting loved ones isn't the violation of personal boundaries it would be in a grown person; it's an expression of affection based on the love stories that were passed down to them early in life. During the tending years, the love stories of babyhood will reemerge and transform as preschoolers begin to form their own ideas about bodies and relationships. The catch? They won't want to tell these stories alone. During the tending years I believe the children we care for will look to us to continue the practice of narration by *scaffolding* the love stories they tell.

Scaffolding, or structuring, is the verbal and physical guidance that adults offer children to support them as they learn, helping them as they grow in their ability to relate to others on their own. In the tending years, scaffolding allows us to listen deeply to the preschoolers we love and to work collaboratively with them to enrich the stories they tell about themselves through their behavior. What specific stories will they tell? Here are three examples.

The New Love Stories of Rough-and-Tumble Play

We are connected: a collaborative love story about doing together

Talk to preschoolers about their social connections and they almost always mention play. "I like them because they race with me," a child might say, or "They're my friend because we swing together." During the tending years, many children will experiment with connecting with peers much the same way they once did with caregivers, using their bodies to communicate their pleasure and enthusiasm at being together. Gone is most of the "gentle but vigorous" play of infancy; in its place is the rambunctious and risky play that so many grown-ups despise. **While rough-and-tumble interactions might look vastly different in the preschool years than they did in babyhood, the story they tell is the same:** *physical closeness is emotional closeness.*

As caregivers, it can be hard to understand the speeding, bouncing, and crashing ways in which so many kids prefer to interact as stories about connection and friendship. (We may have witnessed too many skinned knees and tear-stained faces to believe that this kind of play results in anything but pain.) But what if the minor injuries and hurt feelings that are often the result of rough-and-tumble play weren't something to avoid, but something to draw attention to? What if they're necessary and enriching parts of the connection story?

By providing opportunities to navigate tricky social scenarios like taking responsibility and making amends, the more complicated aspects of physical play can help expand a child's stories about *doing together* to include sentiments like "We are friends because we help each other" and "Together we can make things better." We unknowingly scaffold these new stories every time we model practical ways to show empathy and care or provide language that helps children understand another's perspective. Over time, this co-created story will help the children we care for become better friends, neighbors, and members of their communities.

We are capable: a collaborative love story
about building skills

Much of the play behavior caregivers encounter during the tending years has an air of danger about it. Watching preschoolers at play can cause us to wonder, wincing, when they'll go too fast or too far, when they'll fall. It's all too tempting to tell kids to slow down, to be careful, and often we do. But despite our concerns, many preschoolers continue to take risks in play, experimenting to find out what their bodies can do. **Spiritually, we could understand this experimentation as a trust-building exercise with themselves—a way to gain confidence and skills.** "Through play," early childhood educator Kisha Reid tells us in the documentary series Teachers Speak Out, "children are learning that they are able." As they navigate their own abilities and learn what they're capable of, many kids tell stories of power and triumph. *I did it!* their actions say. *I am strong and brave.*

Caregivers naturally scaffold these stories when we encourage risky play and mirror a child's sense of achievement in words. "Wow," we say, "I saw that! You went so fast!" or "Look at you! Last week, you couldn't go that far—I can tell you've really been practicing!" In our words, the kids we love hear that we believe in them, which helps them believe in themselves.

We are brave: a collaborative love story about letting go of fear

From time to time, rough-and-tumble play will likely result in the consequence many caregivers fear: a child getting hurt. For many adults, this inevitable outcome may feel like a reason to avoid rough-and-tumble play altogether, but for preschoolers, it's all part of the learning experience. After their tears are dried, they're often back to doing the exact same activity that caused the injury in the first place. Why? **During the tending years, one of the purposes of rough-and-tumble play is to help preschoolers practice risk-assessment skills and to learn to trust what their own bodies can do—** to slowly move away from apprehension and toward confidence. *Can I go that fast?* they ask themselves. *Can I climb that high?* With time and practice, kids will find that the answer is very often yes.

For caregivers, rough-and-tumble play also provides a chance to move away from apprehension. Once upon a time—not so very long ago at all—they were fragile and vulnerable, poor decision-makers who needed our guidance at all times. Their play always involved us. Once kids reach the preschool years, it increasingly does not, and we may find ourselves facing feelings of foreboding and alarm. One way we scaffold in these situations is merely to stand back—to allow the risk-taking that may result in injury and to show that we trust the kids in our care just as much as they are learning to trust themselves.

THE WAY TO NARRATION

*Two Ways You Might Already Be Engaged
in This Spiritual Practice*

1. Watching and listening to guide

Many caregivers grew up in cultures where rough-and-tumble play was limited or not allowed at all. If you're making room for the rambunctious and risky in the lives of the children you care for even when you feel doubtful, afraid, or overwhelmed, and if you're watching and listening for opportunities to support them when needed, you're well on your way to using the practice of narration in ways that support their growth. It may be challenging—in some cases immensely so—but keep going!

2. Using your words

In the earliest part of a child's life, the majority of the narrating we do as caregivers is nonverbal. Later, as the children we love become preschoolers, our narration often takes the form of actual words as we reaffirm the original love stories they learned from adults and collaborate to tell new ones that will help them as they grow. When we do this, we ensure that narration becomes a regular part of children's lives and give them language to convey to us the ways in which they might need adult support.

Coming Up Next

In the next two chapters, we'll be investigating how two other varieties of play—pretend play and independent play—offer kids the opportunity to show us who they are. Before we move on to those chapters, please take a moment to answer the questions below in whatever way works best for you.

Reflection Questions

1. What stories are the preschoolers you care for telling through play?

2. Where can you find opportunities to provide scaffolding around play? In what ways are you already doing this?

3. How do you think the culture in which you were raised affects your view of rough-and-tumble play?

Chapter Five

Improvisation

Pretend

If you've "played pretend" with a preschooler recently, you may have had the mind-bending experience of needing to keep up with a story or scenario whose details are increasingly surreal . . . or the mind-numbing experience of trying to stay interested in a story or scenario whose details never change and which you've played approximately eight thousand times before. Both situations are common and frustrating for caregivers to navigate. How, we wonder, are we supposed to behave during these sorts of interactions? Is it normal that the stories so often make no sense? Is it okay that they repeat? And why does the child I care for so often tell me I'm "doing it wrong"?

As with so many of the behaviors that caregivers commonly encounter during the preschool years, I believe the controlling, often completely baffling behaviors that often surface during pretend play offer us the opportunity to understand the preschoolers we love in new ways. In order to understand what they mean, we need to be receptive to all they have to teach us. The good news? We already have the skills to do this, and we've been practicing for longer than we think!

Wing It

No matter how long you've been acting as a caregiver, there will come a moment when (despite how well you know the kids you care for, despite the number of books you may have read or the amount of advice you've received) you will have no idea what you're doing or how to respond. While this moment will probably not feel playful to you, it will rely on one of the main ingredients of play and a skill that you've been honing your whole life: the ability to wing it. While most of us probably don't think of improvisation as a sacred act, it's at the heart of each of the four hidden spiritual practices we've examined so far—curiosity, companionship, replenishment, and narration. To engage in these practices together is essentially to wing it over and over again—to continually invent and reinvent things as we go along, making holy the act of listening and responding to those we love.

As with the other spiritual practices we're examining in this book, the hidden practice of improvisation, which I define as the act of connecting through joyful, spontaneous co-creation, shows up much earlier than we may expect it to and will influence the behavior we encounter later in childhood. It's different from some of the other practices we're talking about, however, in that they are led by adults, but when it comes to improvisation kids will lead the way. Whether we realize it or not, they'll act as spiritual teachers of delight and model for us three habits that enhance our ability to enjoy the time we have with the ones we love: the habit of openness, the habit of attention, and the habit of flexibility. How do these habits tend to show up in the children we care for? Let's consider them one at a time.

The habit of openness

Children are born into a world that is completely new to them. From the very first moments of life, they're absorbing it all: the feel of the air on their skin, the faces and voices of the adults who are called to care for them, the ambient, everyday noises of the place where they now live. As babies take in the world, we caregivers are also taking them in—marveling at their responses, noticing with awe that, somehow, they've grown and changed since yesterday. (How, we wonder, have they grown and changed since *yesterday*?)

If you've experienced it, you know that watching a newborn adjust to life on earth can be a startling, deeply sacred experience that inspires us to interpret the world we live in in new ways. Day after day, their openness will inspire our own, calling us to pay renewed attention to the seemingly mundane details of daily life . . . and, although we're likely not aware of it, prepare us to play with them later on.

The habit of flexibility

In a 2011 article for *Slate*, developmental psychologist Alison Gopnik writes that "we learn differently as children than as adults. For grown-ups," she says, "learning a new skill is painful, attention-demanding, and slow. Children learn unconsciously and effortlessly." This effortlessness is due in part to what's known as *neuroplasticity*, or the brain's ability to physically change as it takes in information. While adult brains are also plastic, or flexible, the brains of young children are especially so. As caregivers, we're constantly presenting the children we love with what's called *novel stimuli*— everything from new words to new foods to new people and experiences. A child's natural ability to integrate these things into their understanding of the world will show up in many places, but it will be in play that we discover the most direct evidence of their inherent flexibility—and where they will call us to continue to develop our own.

The habit of attention

Like every human being, babies are drawn to the bright and the interesting. All day long, infants pay attention—but not necessarily the way we caregivers assume they do. As adults, we often think of "paying attention" as meaning "focusing on one particular thing for a sustained period of time," but in infants and kids, attention doesn't work that way. Instead, their attention is indiscriminate, scanning and resting on anything at all that appeals to them, from motes of dust to ordinary household objects to the behaviors of the people around them.

Later, when we consider their pretend play, we may notice a wide variety of situations and dialogue that have been stitched together, dreamlike, from the stuff of life. Seemingly everything they've noticed and experienced will show up again as fodder for fun—and learning.

Follow the Leader

Caregivers of babies are called to act as guides as the children navigate a world organized by adults. Although this necessary guidance will continue for many years to come, during the tending years many preschoolers will attempt to turn the tables on us by deciding to act as guides to worlds *they* have created, introducing us to new scenarios and casts of characters imagined by them and them alone.

For many caregivers, accompanying a preschooler into a world of their own making can be a struggle. What are we supposed to make of the often plotless, tremendously boring (yet also chaotic) stories they tell? How do we deal with the quick, often nonsensical changes? Most of all, how do we deal with the discomfiting sensation of not being in charge? As adults, many of us take for granted the ability to be in control, but in a child's world we have no control. What do we do with that?

I believe the answer is baked into the play itself. If we look closely at a child's pretend play in all its bizarre glory, we might be able to discover the same habits of improvisation that they modeled for us in infancy. Years after they first started to model the concepts for us, preschoolers continue to use openness, flexibility, and attention in ways that enhance their ability to connect with us—and they'll look to us to do the same. In child development terms, they're looking to us to be what's called *play responsive*: to participate in play while allowing them to take the lead. When we do this, we show that we're flexible enough to move out of our own experience and into a world of the child's making. **During the tending years, improvisation is delight in action: our way of showing that we are willing to go where the children we love go—even to the deepest reaches of their imaginations.** Their play behavior asks three things of us, things that will stretch us into the responsive playmates they crave.

1. Will you accept the premise?

Anyone who's ever played pretend with a preschooler will have had the experience of being expected to accept that something (a stuffed bear, a stick of string cheese, a ball) is actually something else (a queen, a flute, a moon) and then, without warning, likely something else again (a doctor, a magic wand, a tomato). Over and over, the kids we love will offer us the opportunity to improvise by asking us to play along with scenarios that make no literal sense. When we indicate we're open to shifting on the fly—as we often instinctively do—we show the kids we love that we're open to learning about the world they have made and also, by extension, about them and their inner lives.

2. Will you be corrected?

Adults who are engaged in pretend play with preschoolers are often surprised (and, let's be honest, annoyed) by how often they're told they're wrong. You say you like the cake only to find out that it's not a cake at all but a pillow; you reply to a child's assertion that it's a beautiful day only to be told with a disconcerting amount of ferocity that it's suddenly not a beautiful day at all because the living room is actually being destroyed by earthquakes and tornadoes. Why do kids want so badly to play with us only to tell us that we're mistaken?

In the tending years, kids ask us to be as mentally flexible as they often must be—exploring by trial and error, and often being helped and corrected by a person in a position of authority. (If we didn't realize before how much of the help we provide to young children comes in the form of correction, pretend play will quickly inform us.) As the ultimate authority on the imaginary worlds they create, many kids are thrilled to have the opportunity to tell us what's what—and unsurprisingly, they'll take the chance as often as they can. When we stretch into the practice of improvisation and demonstrate our willingness to be wrong—a difficult thing for many adults, myself included, to consider—we show them we're willing to live in their worlds the way they live in ours: ready to reassess what they think they know at a moment's notice.

3. Will you join them in their world?

Most caregivers know in theory that the kids we love are watching and learning from our behavior, but the details of what they're observing often remain something of a mystery until they begin to show up in pretend play. In his book *Through the Children's Gate*, writer Adam Gopnik, brother of Alison Gopnik, tells the story of his then three-year-old daughter Olivia, whose imaginary friend is a man so busy he's never available to play with her. "He canceled lunch. Again," Adam quotes Olivia sighing—a spot-on parody of an exasperated grown-up whose friends have too much on their plates to have time to socialize.

When a concerned Adam calls Alison, she tells him not to fret. "She's putting a name on a series of manners," Alison says—in other words, using pretend play to describe the habits of the people around her. Like novelists, many preschoolers create vivid but fictional worlds based on the stuff of real life, including the behavior of loved ones. Olivia, a keen observer of life in early twenty-first-century New York City, incorporated her family's all-consuming busyness into her play. Kids living in other circumstances may incorporate different, less harried scenarios into theirs. **No matter the inspiration they're drawing from, we can think of** the imaginary worlds and friendships created by the preschoolers we love as an invitation to join them— and to learn more about them along the way.

THE WAY TO IMPROVISATION

Two Ways You Might Already Be Engaged in This Spiritual Practice

1. Saying "yes, and"

Lovers of improv comedy will know that one of the most famous guidelines of improv is to respond to any new scenario with the words "yes, and." In his book of that title, Kelly Leonard, an executive director of the Second City comedy enterprise, tells us that these two simple words drastically improve our ability to relate to others. "When we are in full improvisor mode," he says, "we become better leaders and better followers; likewise, we hear things that we didn't hear before because we are listening deeply and fully in the moment." In caregiving, the capacity to say "yes, and"—to accept a child's invitation to fully participate in pretend play—opens for us a hundred ways to know the kids we care for as exactly who they are. If you're striving to do this despite the many challenges involved, feel proud and keep going—whether they say so or not, the kids you love will appreciate it!

2. Staying receptive

"The moment I decided to follow instead of lead," said Head Start founder Janet Gonzalez-Mena, "I discovered the joys of becoming part of a small child's world." While Gonzalez-Mena makes the decision sound easy, for many caregivers it is quite the opposite. They must choose to be play responsive again and again, as they strive to refrain from correcting the child in their care, or conveying their (completely understandable) boredom or exasperation to them. If you're consistently trying to follow a child's lead in play even when it's challenging, you'll likely find it easier to follow their lead in other ways as well, affirming them both in and outside of play.

Coming Up Next

In the next chapter, our last on play, we'll be considering the fun preschoolers have all by themselves . . . and how caregivers can make room for (and honor) a child's capacity for flow. Before you move on, please take a moment to answer the following reflection questions in the way that makes the most sense to you.

Reflection Questions

1. If the preschoolers you care for engage in pretend play, what form does it tend to take? What does their play tell you about the kind of things they're interested in?

2. What aspects of "real life" are the preschoolers you love incorporating into their pretend play? What does this tell you about the sorts of things they notice?

3. Where do you find yourself struggling to enter a child's world? Where does it come easily for you?

Chapter Six

Immersion

Seems Like Play

"I celebrate myself and sing myself." Walt Whitman wasn't a preschooler when he wrote these words. But with this one poetic line, he perfectly captured a young child's way of being in the world. If you've ever seen a kid you care for face a fear or conquer a long-standing challenge—completing a puzzle or reaching the top of the play structure, for instance—you've probably noticed the joy that lights up their face when they realize they did it. You may have even heard or seen them crow some version of the words "I did it!"

At the root of this joy is an activity many caregivers don't even consider preschoolers to be capable of: contemplation. It's easy to understand why we adults would be suspicious of a child's ability to engage in something we consider to be challenging even for us— after all, we think, their attention spans are short, their energy tends to run high . . . and can they even be quiet for that long? The truth is that in preschoolers, contemplation doesn't have the silent, almost religious quality that many adults associate with it. It doesn't usually involve stillness, and it's often far from tranquil. Instead, in preschoolers, contemplation tends to be active. It seems like play—the kind they're drawn to independently, that they return to again and again— and I believe it's an integral part of their spiritual development. But how can caregivers make room for and support this development in a world that threatens to teach us (and the kids we love) that contemplation is a waste of time?

During the tending years, I believe the preschoolers we love will offer us a gift we didn't know we needed: the opportunity to observe and honor their unique, innate sense of focus and fun by watching, listening to, and supporting forms of play that may look very different from what we might expect.

Going Deep

If we watch carefully, we can see that almost every child has a form of play that they're especially drawn to, one so endlessly interesting that they can engage in it over and over again. I consider this meditative, often repetitive interest-based play part of the practice of immersion. In immersion, human beings—including even the very youngest kids—"go deep" in something so engaging that we lose track of everything else. As a practice, immersion is unique because it's personal— it looks different for each person engaged in it. In kids, it can take innumerable forms. Some want to wear their tutu or superhero cape every day. Some want to line up their cars in perfectly straight lines. Some want to pursue the same physical challenge as many times as it takes to get it exactly right. While these types of play appear to be completely different, they're all part of immersion because they fulfill the same sacred needs: the need for autonomy, the need to focus on something of interest, and the need for meaningful challenge.

Unlike the other types of play we've examined so far in this chapter, which tend to involve others, immersion is not about others at all, but about the self. *What has caught my attention? How do I want to engage with it? What can I learn or accomplish here?* Even in babyhood, kids choose activities and playthings according to their answers to these questions, practicing immersion instinctively.

As we observe the kids we love engaged in the practice of immersion, we may notice three aspects that make it different from other types of play.

Three Traits of Immersive Play

1. Immersive play is self-assigned

Although we caregivers mostly aren't apt to think of it this way, to watch an infant at play is to see a person making a series of decisions about how to interact with the world. Before they're even one year old, many babies choose independent, thoroughly absorbing *play tasks* that will allow them to engage with something in the immediate environment that has drawn their attention—and as we learned in the last chapter, everything has the potential to draw a baby's attention! To the majority of adults, the self-assigned play tasks of infants don't necessarily seem like fun, but for babies, they couldn't be more enjoyable. Watching the wind in the trees, banging two measuring cups together, tasting the fuzz on the carpet—these seemingly mundane activities meet the literal definition of fun because, for the very young, they're what psychologist Travis Tae Oh calls "experiences of liberating engagement." By choosing activities that stimulate their senses and teach them more about the world, even very young children find the happiness that comes from freely selecting that which interests them.

2. Immersive play is self-directed

While adults are usually present during immersive play, we are not in charge of it. (As we'll discuss later, the practice of immersion isn't ours to take part in; it's only ours to observe and affirm.) Instead of relying on caregivers to show them what to do, babies and toddlers themselves may make and follow a set of repetitive rhythms and rules—officially called *play schemas*—that govern how they'll engage with whatever has caught their attention. These play schemas are often invisible to caregivers unless we've learned to look for them, but they make up a huge portion of the play done by very young children as they learn about the world around them. If you've spent a lot of time with young children, you may recognize some of these common schemas:

- *transport play* (moving objects from one place to another)

- *connecting play* (stacking or joining things together and then dismantling them)
- *trajectory play* (throwing or tossing things)
- *enclosure play* (creating boundaries or shelters)

To caregivers who are unfamiliar with the concept of play schemas, many of these activities look like the stuff of mess, noise, and general chaos. But for many babies and toddlers, they're often incredibly satisfying. Why? Schemas allow children to move into their power: to experiment, to make plans and carry them out, even to create and destroy. As they grow into the preschool years, schemas will offer new and exciting ways to engage with the world around them.

3. Immersive play leads to self-forgetting

If you've ever lost track of time while learning a new skill or working on a challenging project, you've experienced *self-forgetting*, also known as *flow*. Mihaly Csikszentmihalyi, the psychologist widely considered to be the first person to study the concept of flow states, defines them in his book *Flow* as moments when "a person's body or mind is stretched to its limits in a voluntary effort to accomplish something difficult and worthwhile." During flow experiences, we are so absorbed in learning, observing, or accomplishing the task at hand that the world around us, and even our very selves, seem to disappear.

Although Csikszentmihalyi himself didn't study flow experiences in kids, other psychologists and child development researchers have noticed that flow is evident in very young children's play activity. Lori A. Custodero, professor of music education at Teachers College, Columbia University, notes in her paper "Observing Flow in Young Children's Music Learning" that in kids' flow states, "thinking and doing become one" as the activity they're engaged in "becomes the most compelling aspect of their immediate world." When engaged in flow, even infants appear to display obliviousness (losing awareness of those around them as they fix their attention on whatever they've chosen to do) and satisfaction (expressing pleasure when they've accomplished the outcome they desire).

In later years, the self-forgetting aspect of immersive play is the one caregivers are most likely to notice.

As children grow, self-assignment, self-direction, and self-forgetting will remain integral to their practice of immersion, even as it shifts to take on new, more complicated forms. During the preschool years, I believe these traits challenge us to honor the desire and ability of the kids we love to play independently. Many of us will find it difficult to meet this challenge, because it will require us to hold back in ways we may not be used to. Unlike several of the other practices we're examining in this book, which are best done by caregiver and child together, immersion requires an entirely different sort of response from adults: not to participate at all.

Watch and Learn

As caregivers, many of us have internalized the idea that the best, safest, most educational and satisfying play a preschooler can engage in is play arranged and orchestrated by adults. We can't be blamed for this assumption—after all, young children are in frequent need of help, guidance, and supervision. Isn't it just easier for everyone if caregivers preemptively offer all of these as often as we can?

During the tending years, many of the kids we love will ask us to question this assumption. They do so by choosing play activities that most of us would never choose. Instead of asking us to practice immersion *with* them, the preschoolers we care for will ask us, through their behavior, to practice its mirror image *beside* them: witnessing. Witnessing means openheartedly observing a child's way of being in the world. It corresponds to what child development experts call *non-intrusiveness*: the capacity to be available to support a child's interactions and explorations without being overly involved in them.

To effectively practice witnessing, we must do one thing: sit back and watch. I believe that the opportunity to witness immersion is one of the most profound gifts we are offered during the tending years. **If we allow ourselves to simply observe the play of children we** love, we'll realize that, for preschoolers, almost any activity can be immersive, challenging, and fun— and tell us more about who they are and what they like. When the kids we care for engage in deep, absorbing play in our presence, they show us what they notice, what they're drawn to, what inner needs they're striving to meet, their innate definition of fun.

During the tending years, caregivers are likely to find that several of the play schemas that first appear in infants are combining into new forms of immersive play, each one filling a specific spiritual need and requiring from us a specific type of witnessing.

The Three Types of Immersive Play— and How We Witness Them

1. Soothing and satisfying play

When my daughter was two and three years old, she loved to "play beans." "Playing beans" consisted of dumping a plastic sack of dry eighteen-bean soup mix into a Pyrex baking dish and then simply shifting the beans around—raking them with a dinner fork, running them through her fingers, hauling them in the back of a tiny dump truck. This was sometimes connected to a pretend play scenario with some elements of plot—"Oh, no! This load of rocks has fallen all over the highway! We have to clean them up!"—but it frequently involved play for its own sake: running the beans through her fingers, sorting them into piles by color or shape, making patterns from them.

The most effective way many of us already witness this kind of soothing, absorbing play with the kids we love is simply by not interrupting it. Because this type of play grows from a spiritual need for calm and focus, caregivers may notice that for some children, particularly autistic kids, it's more absorbing than other types of play. When we let kids play until their own interest in the activity is extinguished, we teach them that their choices and spiritual needs matter to us.

2. Practice and mastery play

While my daughter was drawn again and again to the meditation of bean play, her best friend was most emphatically not. (When invited to sort lentils with her, he would sink to the floor and audibly groan with dismay at the idea that this could be fun.) For him, the practice of immersion looked like movement: trying over and over again to make it to the end of the playground's balance beam, monkey bars, or soccer field. For many kids, "going deep" in a challenge like this—one that requires a great deal of concentration and physical persistence—meets their spiritual need for challenge and satisfaction. For them, immersive play is goal-oriented.

Caregivers practicing witness beside this type of play will notice that many kids ask for validation as they try and try and try again. "Look at me!" they might say. "Look, look, I'm doing it!" Every time we affirm a child's progress without suggesting new ways to improve or be more careful, we honor their need to figure out on their own how they might attain their goals.

3. Experimental play

It is a truth of the tending years that for many kids, immersive play can seem a bit like mischief: throwing toys, smearing paint, making other assorted messes. Although caregivers are frequently frustrated by behaviors like this (raise your hand if you've been there), they're just as absorbing for preschoolers as the other, less chaotic forms of immersion because they engage the senses, allow for deeper focus, and offer a sense of challenge.

Effectively witnessing this type of play can be exceedingly hard for some caregivers. The good news is that witnessing doesn't mean violating our own boundaries. As we'll discuss in a moment, one of the most helpful ways we witness experimental play is by setting limits on where and how it can be done. Setting limits on experimental play ("We only do bubbles outside"; "Play dough stays on the tray") helps kids naturally integrate those limits into their own play.

THE WAY TO IMMERSION AND WITNESS

Two Ways You Might Already Be Engaged in These Spiritual Practices

1. Holding back

Like many things young children do, immersive play often doesn't make much sense to grown people. We may find ourselves worrying about it, even trying to prevent it. *They must be bored*, we might think, watching even a one-year-old return to the same activity again and again. *Am I entertaining them enough? Maybe I should entertain them more.* To deal with our own discomfort with watching the kids we love do things that, to adult minds, seem boring or odd, we're often tempted to increase the level of engagement we offer: to show them a new toy, to put on a show. While this type of intervention is tempting, resisting it can help the kids we love develop their capacities for attention and joy.

In addition, allowing independent, immersive play of a child's own choosing affirms for them that their interests are valid and worthy. As they grow and their interests inevitably change, our affirmation will stay with them and they may feel more free to continue sharing their interests with us.

2. **Making a "yes space"**

One of the most common reasons caregivers hesitate to support immersive play is the idea that it may be messy or dangerous. As caregivers of the very young, we tend to worry that the world is littered with choking hazards, stain-attracting clothes and furniture, and plain old dirt.

The creation of either a temporary or permanent "yes space" (a term that comes from early childhood educator Janet Lansbury, herself a strong advocate for young children's capacity to play independently) can help allay our fears. A "yes space" is any environment where kids can safely engage in play without getting hurt, damaging furniture, or making messes. If you've ever covered a table with a sheet of newsprint before painting or brought certain toys into the park or yard, you've already created a "yes space" . . . and given yourself the ability to witness play without concern!

Coming Up Next

In the next and final section of this book, Rest, we'll be examining three hidden spiritual practices related to rest: presence, consistency, and peace. Before you move on to that section, please take some time to answer the questions below in whatever way works for you.

Reflection Questions

1. What forms of immersive play do you notice the preschoolers you love engaging in?

2. In what ways do you find yourself supporting immersive play? In what ways do you find supporting it to be a challenge?

3. If the kids you care for are drawn to immersive play and you haven't already created a "yes space," what could you do to make a temporary one? List some ideas.

Part Three

Rest

Marco, age two, still needs a nap, but often refuses to take one. Every day at his designated rest time, he kicks and screams and flails and then, exhausted, finally passes out wherever he happens to be: on the floor, at the table while eating a snack, even in the cat bed! His parents wonder if there's anything they can do to make it easier for him to get the rest he needs during the day.

Although they have their own cozy bed to nap in, Pax, four, will only have their desperately needed "rest time" on the couch in the living room with an adult beside them. Why, their family asks, can't they sleep independently? Should they be trying harder to make Pax rest?

Brooklyn, five, won't lie down on her nap mat at school unless she knows exactly what's happening next. All afternoon, she questions the adults around her about the next thing on the schedule and will not settle into any activity until she gets the answers she craves. What, her teachers ask each other, should they do?

Eli, who's three, will not go to bed without their special blanket, a glass of water, and exactly eight kisses. Although their grandmother goes along with this routine when she's caring for them, it's very different (and much more complicated!) than the one she used with her own kids and she often finds herself questioning, with no small amount of exasperation, whether all this is strictly necessary.

If you've worked with preschoolers for any length of time, you know that rest doesn't always come easy. As caregivers, we understand that downtime is essential to a child's well-being, so we do everything we can to ensure that they get enough rest to play and grow. We prioritize naps, build elaborate bedtime routines, and bring all our creativity and enthusiasm to convincing kids that lying down in the cozy spot we've designed just for them is a great idea. And then . . . well . . .

It's an unfortunate fact of life that children often feel very differently about the concept of rest than their caregivers do. For many of them, the day seems to be a never-ending quest to resist any sort of downtime, no matter how tired they are. Which leaves us wondering: how are we meant to handle these weary but often overstimulated kids? And why—*why*—do so many of the preschoolers we care for seem to hate the idea of relaxing so very much?

As a longtime caregiver of preschool-age kids, I've asked myself these questions more times than I can count. Over time, I've also come to realize that, like so many of the adult notions I've come to take for granted, my idea of what is restful doesn't necessarily align with a preschooler's.

Throughout this book, we've learned that young children's behaviors help us rethink the care we offer them and expand our understanding of the world to include theirs. As we'll discuss in the next three chapters, rest is no exception. During the tending years, I believe that the kids we love will push us to go beyond what we think we know and to have confidence that the three types of spiritual rest we instinctively offer them from the very start of life—presence, consistency, and peace—are, in their own ways, just as restorative and protective as the sleep so many of us try so hard to convince them to enjoy.

Like previous sections of this book, this final section offers three chapters that will introduce you to various aspects of each hidden practice: where it comes from, how the preschoolers you care for might ask you to engage with it, and the ways you are already providing the spiritual teaching they need.

Chapter Seven

Presence

Together

There's no way for me to know for sure what sentence I said most often as a full-time caregiver of young children, but the top contender is this one: "Let's just rest here together." Every weekday for two decades, in classrooms and homes, beside cribs and cots and nap mats, these six words were my go-to when trying to convince preschoolers to take an often desperately needed afternoon rest. Did this sentence work all the time, reliably enticing even the most overtired three-year-old to fall into a deep and restorative slumber? Of course not. But it did help children rest much of the time, and although it took me the better part of twenty years to realize why, I believe I finally do: it contained the word *together*.

By now, we already know that the preschoolers we love prioritize their connection to beloved adults above all other things. During the tending years, kids' desire to be close to caregivers physically and emotionally affects everything: how they eat, what they play, how they learn to interact with others. Unsurprisingly, it also affects their understanding of rest, and long before the tending years begin, their understanding will begin to shape our own in ways that will invisibly but thoroughly prepare us to nurture them as they grow.

Presence and Absence

In his book *Four Thousand Weeks: Time Management for Mortals*, *Guardian* reporter Oliver Burkeman writes movingly of his experiences with his young son. "He was sheer presence," Burkeman writes, "participating unconditionally in the moment in which he found himself, and I wanted to join him in it." Like many caregivers, Burkeman noticed that the more time he spent with his child, the more his child's way of being in the world shifted his own. While this reciprocal influence will be felt again and again over the course of a child's development, one of the first times adults tend to notice it is when their infant is sleeping. If you've ever been lucky enough to hold a sleeping baby, you know that sleeping babies are in possession of a magical power: simply by existing, they inspire other people to physical and mental stillness. Writer Dave Mosher, chronicling his own experience with what he calls the "baby high," reports in a piece for *Business Insider* that carrying his dozing two-month-old in a baby sling "enhances [his] experience of living in the moment while engaging a grab-bag of pleasurable senses." Being physically close to his daughter, he says, "can trigger a satisfying, heartfelt glow." While not every caregiver feels the glow to the extent that Mosher seems to, experts he spoke to for the article told him that many people report feeling increased levels of positive (and restful) emotions like calmness when in the presence of sleeping babies.

For however long a baby sleeps, the person who's holding them has only one task, one thing to practice, and that is the "sheer presence" Burkeman writes of, mirroring the child's tranquility. In these moments governed by slumber, we are not our to-do list, our worries, or our responsibilities. Instead, we are breath and heartbeat and skin, wholly, completely, and unconditionally here for the child we love, for as long as they need us.

For many, this moment is a revelation. The first time we practice presence with a child we love, everything around us seems to stop. The world falls away. What is this feeling? At first, true presence might feel so unfamiliar that we may only recognize it for all it is not.

True presence is the absence of hurry

Caregivers' ability to be in the here-and-now is often strained by all we have to accomplish in the day. Yes, we've probably read about mindfulness; maybe we've watched or listened to TED talks about stress and self-care. But for many—particularly those caring for multiple kids, those who have no support from other caregivers, and those who are living with disability or neurodivergence—mindfulness and self-care may seem out of reach. We have so much to prepare, arrange, organize, and clean (the dishes in the sink, the toys on the floor, the never-ending laundry and lunches, the playdates and doctors' appointments) that the pressure to rush from responsibility to responsibility is immense. Until, that is, the baby falls asleep. For the amount of time the baby naps, whether it's for five minutes or forty, we have only one job: to keep that baby sleeping. Everything else can wait. Whether we want them to or not, infants have a way of forcing us into something like serenity—a power that I believe will last long after they grow beyond babyhood and enter the tending years.

True presence is the absence of separation

For weeks or months after birth, infants around the world will get much of their sleep on, with, or close to a caregiver. Irrevocably, the majority of them come to associate rest with the bodies of beloved people: the gentle rise and fall of a parent's chest, the scent of a relative's perfume, the sound of a sibling breathing nearby. **Just by being near them during their first experiences of rest, we teach the babies in our care that *connection is rest*—that it's in proximity to others that we are able to feel the most at ease not only in our bodies, but in our minds and spirits as well.**

True presence is the absence of resentment

It's a fact of life with young children that our schedules and plans will be interrupted from time to time by minor inconveniences. As babies grow toward toddlerhood, sleep itself can become a source of aggravation for many caregivers. The baby is fussy and won't settle the way they usually do; they keep waking up despite our soothing interventions; they took a brief car or stroller nap that precludes the possibility of any other sleep for the rest of the day—examples are endless.

Despite the general unpredictability of many infants' sleep patterns (and despite our own tendency to feel frustrated by this), the majority of caregivers strive instinctively not to let our irritation get the better of us in front of the children we love. Whether we realize it or not, this instinctive striving is one of the hallmarks of presence. Child development researchers call it *non-hostility*: the ability to avoid conveying feelings like boredom, frustration, or exasperation to children in our care, even when things are indisputably boring, frustrating, or exasperating.

When we show non-hostility—responding to mishaps, disruptions, and changes with equanimity and kindness (and without blame or anger)—we create environments that are inherently restful for children because they are low in stress and conflict. Over time, the environment we create affects a child's ability not only to sleep soundly, but to be able to relax into rest when they need to.

Sleep versus Rest

What I've come to call the practice of presence is also known in child development circles as *emotional availability.* **When we caregivers are emotionally available to the children we love, able to be present with and for them, kids become able to trust in our ability to reassure and comfort.** What begins in infancy with literal sleep will become, during the tending years, a general confidence in us and our ability to be there for them when they need us. In her book *Rest, Play, Grow*, attachment theory expert Deborah MacNamara calls this confidence the ability to *rest in our care*, and during the preschool period it will influence children's behavior around sleep and relaxation. And we will be pushed not only to compassionately respond to their need for rest, but also to rethink our definition of it.

Although adults often consider *rest* and *sleep* to be synonyms, I've come to believe that for many preschoolers, they are actually two distinct things. While sleep is a biological necessity that helps them recover from learning and playing, for many children it feels like a rupture: a long separation from those they love, who disappear when they close their eyes. Rest, on the other hand, is a spiritual concept based not in separation but in feelings of connection, comfort, safety, and a general sense of certainty that we will be there when they need us. **For the majority of preschoolers, sleep is separation. Rest is reassurance.**

Many, many caregivers will at some point find themselves working with a visibly exhausted child who refuses to even consider resting in any way. In at least some of these situations, their reluctance may be based on these different definitions. Because a preschooler may naturally equate naps with distance, they won't take one; because the caregiver equates sleep with rest, they press harder to make the nap happen, initiating a power struggle and escalating conflict. During the tending years, I believe that preschoolers will show us, if we pay attention, how well the practice of presence (and our own emotional availability) can help them recover from the physical and mental exertion of learning and growing and how to separate the concepts of sleep and rest. Predictably, they'll use every device in their behavioral toolbox to try to communicate to us how deeply we affect their ability to rest . . . and to ask us to be more emotionally available.

How Do Preschoolers Request Presence and Emotional Availability?

Extended nap times and bedtimes
Some of the kids we love will ask us to practice presence with them by making the transitions from activity to rest last as long as possible. They'll ask for glasses of water, stuffed animals, extra songs or stories, kisses, anything that will keep a caregiver with them for the longest possible period of time. When we're tempted to rush through these transitions, preschoolers will remind us that presence is the absence of hurry by ensuring a slowness that feels restful to them and that guarantees both our physical and emotional availability.

While it can often feel like it, preschoolers who are engaging in what I call *extension behavior* aren't trying to make our days more difficult or to deprive us of the break we so desperately need. Instead, I believe, they're merely trying to create the ideal conditions in which to recover from the strain of learning, playing, and navigating a world that is completely new to them. For the majority of preschoolers, recovery and respite will continue to require the company of a loving adult. **For them, we *are* rest.**

Calling out and getting up

During the tending years, many caregivers find that rest does not come easily to preschoolers who are alone. If we think back to the beginning of their lives, when they most often rested with a caregiver nearby, this makes sense. For them, rest once inevitably meant connection. As they grow, however, rest often begins to come with more distance: adults may ask them to sleep in their own bed, on their own nap mat, etc. For some preschoolers this distance can feel enormously stressful, and they'll seek to alleviate the discomfort they feel by calling out, getting up, or engaging in other sorts of *checking behavior* during rest periods to confirm that an adult is nearby.

While this behavior can be undeniably exasperating, I believe it's through checking that preschoolers prompt us to remember that presence is the absence of separation and encourage us to remain in close contact with them while they settle into rest. Over time, as we respond to their desire to be close to us, we may find our reactions softening and our ability to be present improving as we begin to understand their needs in new ways.

Persistence

Many of the behavioral tools preschoolers use to encourage us to practice presence with them, including the two we've explored above, can cause adults no small amount of annoyance. *Really?* we ask ourselves when the child we care for pops out of bed for another snuggle. *Again?* we wonder as they peek around the corner just to see what we're doing. "I can't do this alone," their behavior says. "I need you to help me. Can I rest in your care?"

Over and over, day after day, our capacity to be emotionally available and to practice presence with the preschoolers we love is tested as they persistently call us to understand rest (and life) the way they do—as an opportunity to be together. It's through this continual testing—so exasperating! So time-consuming!—that we are slowly pulled away from resentment and toward greater compassion for their needs and desires. Every time we show up in response to them—every time we ourselves are persistently available and loving despite our annoyance—we build trust between ourselves and the child we care for. This trust will sustain our ability to connect even in the toughest moments.

THE WAY TO PRESENCE

Two Ways You Might Already Be Engaged in This Spiritual Practice

Whether we're consciously aware of it or not, most caregivers already engage in the spiritual practice of presence with the children we care for. Even as we struggle to balance the needs of the preschooler in our care with our own needs—and even as we may still be gaining confidence in our ability to be everything they need us to be—we intuitively find ways big and small to be emotionally available. Here are a couple of small ways in which you're already practicing presence in your days:

1. Preemptive connection

One of the main barriers to practicing presence with the children we care for is the sense that we just don't have the time. We know that many preschoolers crave slowness and closeness around rest periods, but those things take valuable minutes that we may not feel we have—not to mention a great deal of energy just at the moment when we're probably in need of a break! If over time you've realized that transitions around rest are taking longer than you'd like them to, because the child you care for is requesting increased connection, and you've begun to prepare by setting aside time for that connection—even just an extra two minutes—you're showing that you understand how restful your presence can be. Meeting a child's need for closeness with you before they have a chance to request it behaviorally can help them trust that we'll continue to be available even when separated from them by rest.

2. Resting together

Just as they moved us to greater tranquility when they were babies, preschoolers have the power to inspire us to stillness during the tending years by often resting better when we're close to them. If, from time to time, you invite the tired preschooler you care for to rest with you nearby—on the couch while you read a book; in bed while you wait in the corner of the room, etc.—you're instinctively recognizing and meeting their need to rest while connected and helping them trust that you will remain present even while they rest. Not every child needs a caregiver nearby to rest, but if the preschooler you care for prefers it, staying at close range from time to time can help smooth the way to nap time or bedtime.

Coming Up Next

In the next chapter, we'll be examining how the practice of consistency can work together with the practice of presence to help us be available to the kids we love. Before we get there, please take a moment to answer the questions below.

Reflection Questions

1. How do the preschoolers you care for ask you to practice presence with them around periods of rest?

2. Where do you find yourself struggling to practice presence?

3. In what ways are you showing up and practicing presence even when it's challenging for you?

Chapter Eight

Consistency

Emergency!

Back in chapter 3, I mentioned a phrase my then four-year-old daughter had coined to describe the feelings of overwhelm she was apt to feel from time to time: *my brain is going emergency!* Although I've never known another child who used that exact wording, I've cared for many whose actions indicated they were familiar with emergency brain, and you probably have too. Signs of it include crankiness, pushback, meltdowns—a

127

whole range of behaviors that we caregivers commonly struggle to deal with.

Part of the reason "emergency brain" presents such a challenge to caregivers is that it often seems to come out of nowhere. A child who was happily playing just moments ago suddenly falls to the floor weeping. One who was getting ready for bed is now angrily stomping away from us, unable to explain what the problem is. Even if we find ourselves in situations like this on a regular basis (and if we're caring for at least one pre-schooler, we probably do), it's easy to feel flummoxed again and again as we search for solutions. What do they need? How do we help? What do we do now? In the moment, it's hard to know. Luckily, whether we know it or not, caregivers have an array of spiritual tools at our disposal to help the kids we love regain their emotional balance . . . and we've likely been using them for much longer than we realize.

If you've ever read one of the thousands of books targeted at caregivers—and if you're reading this now, you probably have—you've likely received the message that routine is important for kids. Whether you bristled at this assertion or fully embraced it, it's everywhere: child development experts agree that structure helps children thrive. But why exactly is routine so important? **The answer is that for kids, routine is restful.** When adults create a reliable routine, children can be assured that they know what comes next and what is expected of them. For some caregivers, the words *routine* or *structure* may bring to mind charts, schedules, or strict procedures, but the truth is that for most people, a routine doesn't involve any of those things. Instead, the structure kids need most tends to naturally arise out of the spiritual practice of consistency, which I define as the reliable enactment of familiar rituals that help to comfort, soothe, and regulate. Whether we're aware of it or not, nearly all of us already practice consistency with the kids we love through the soothing behaviors that come most naturally to us. From the very beginning of a child's life, caregivers the world over practice consistency by building rituals of soothing sameness with and for the kids they love. These rituals consistently include four elements that I call *connection methods*: closeness, action, language, and mindfulness. Together they form the acronym CALM.

CALM: The Four Connection Methods

1. Closeness

We've seen throughout this book that adults instinctively use physical closeness to connect with the babies we care for. We hold them near, stroke their skin, whisper sweet nothings to them. Although we may not be aware of doing these things in any sort of ritualized way (or even, in some cases, fully aware of doing them at all), it's common for caregivers to use touch to connect at specific, identifiable times, like before and after sleep or during bathing or changing. When we do this, we elevate everyday care tasks—and the transitions between them—from the mundane to the sacred, teaching the children we love that each moment they spend with us has the potential to be special. As we'll discuss later, the association between touch and transitions is a strong one for many young children, and their desire for touch will often affect their behavior when it's time to move from one activity to another.

2. Action

Long before babies are born, they become accustomed to the gentle, rhythmic movement of their gestational parent walking around, going about their daily routine. After they're born, this rhythm will reappear as a baby's caregivers instinctively echo it by carrying, swaying, or rocking them at a speed that resembles the walking movements the baby would have felt in utero. Research into motion-based interactions like these (which are officially called *rhythmic stimulation*) has demonstrated that they have a soothing effect on both adults and babies—when infant and caregiver move together in synchronous fashion, their brain waves, breathing, and heartbeats synchronize too. Over time, both infants and their caregivers tend to associate motion with comfort, reassurance, and care, an association that lasts far into childhood and affects the way we continue to soothe them as they grow.

3. Language

Just as caregivers use rhythmic movement to connect with the babies in their care, we also tend to use rhythmic language. Researchers Daisy Fancourt and Rosie Perkins write in a 2018 study on interactions between infants and children that this special form of "infant-directed speech" consists of "exaggerations, elevated pitch, slow repetitions, and melodic elaborations of ordinary vocal communication"—in other words, of talking that sounds a lot like singing and has a rhythm like that of rocking.

This kind of speech is known as *parentese*, but parents are far from the only people who use it. Many adults naturally employ this form of communication when in the presence of babies, and remnants of it linger in the ways we comfort kids throughout childhood. Some child development theorists, like the child psychologist Colwyn Trevarthen, hypothesize that lullabies (which have been used for at least four thousand years to soothe babies and young children)—may have developed directly out of the singsong quality of this type of speech. As we'll discuss later, language is a preferred connection method for many kids—one that can reliably introduce a feeling of peace whenever it's needed.

4. Mindfulness

In his book *Everyday Blessings*, famed meditation teacher Jon Kabat-Zinn echoes the sentiments of many when he writes that "this moment—any moment, actually—may seem far too ordinary, routine, and fleeting to single out for attention." As adults, many of us spend our time dwelling on the past or trying to predict the future, concerned with any number of things we can't control. But for infants, this moment is all there is. They lock eyes with us, grasp a finger in their starfish hands, and we may suddenly feel just as anchored to the present as they do, experiencing it with them. In other words, practicing mindfulness. Kabat-Zinn defines mindfulness as "awareness that arises through paying attention in the present moment to whatever appears and observing it non-judgmentally and without reactivity." To watch a newborn focus on a face, a toy, a few dust motes floating in a beam of sunlight is to see that babies are mindfulness experts—and what's more, they're experts at pulling us into a state of mindfulness with them, calling us to watch and wonder, thoroughly absorbed for just a second or two in what they're seeing and feeling.

Through our care of the children we love, we practice mindfulness again and again for brief periods without even realizing it. As they grow—and as we grow as caregivers—this skill will help us soothe and center them when they're in need.

Instinctively, those caring for babies combine or layer the four connection elements of closeness, action, language, and mindfulness to create what I call CALM rituals, or soothing routines based in the practice of consistency that use a child's preferred connection methods to help bring them back to a regulated state. In infancy, CALM rituals teach babies that care and comfort are part of the daily routine. During the tending years, I believe that the preschoolers we love continue to strongly associate the elements of CALM with love and connection, and we can use those elements to help smooth transitions between activities and to help guide them back to a regulated state the same way we did when they were small. Unfortunately, the ways in which many of them show that they need this—tantrums, meltdowns, and other indicators of "emergency brain"—can feel overwhelming to many caregivers. Why does this happen, and what can we do?

Always

Those of us who have cared for preschoolers have likely noticed that many of them have a strong desire for sameness and repetition. This desire (and their tendency to experience moments of "emergency brain" when it isn't fulfilled) can be exasperating, but it's also very common. Where does this preference come from? In part, it comes from us. Although our own routines tend to be invisible to us, they are far from invisible to the kids we care for. For years, they've been watching and absorbing every detail of adults' daily lives: they know that we always drink a cup of coffee, always feed the cat, and always water the plants before leaving the house. For many preschoolers, the concept of *always*— so dependable, so soothing—brings a great deal of peace, allowing them to know exactly what's coming and what's expected of them.

Unfortunately, a great many things tend to fall outside the realm of *always*. To the majority of adults, these unpredictable events—schedule changes, the grocery store unexpectedly being out of a crucial dinner ingredient—are a normal if exasperating fact of twenty-first-century life, which we deal with as gracefully as we can. To a preschooler, they can throw the whole world into disarray and the mind into an attack of "emergency brain." Even transitions that seem routine to us, such as the daily shift from daycare to car to home, or from bath to story time to bed, can be fraught with anxiety and conflict, leading to the sort of meltdowns that so confuse caregivers. *What happened?* we ask ourselves. *They were fine a minute ago!*

A tantrum or meltdown or that seems to come out of nowhere is often the result of a shift in the day's plans that may seem minor to a caregiver but (momentarily) disastrous to a child. It strongly communicates their need for *always*, and their frustration that it has been disrupted. What should we do, and how can we help children cope in these moments? The answer is already right in front of us: we can keep CALM.

A CALM Ritual Recipe

During the tending years, the CALM rituals that care-givers instinctively employed to soothe babies will take on new forms. But we will continue to use their favorite connection methods to help the children we love feel safe and cared for. CALM rituals with preschoolers work the same way they did with babies: by layering the connection methods our children already love. They allow us to shift transitions like coming home or going to bed from an overwhelming hassle to an opportunity to *be together* (closeness), *do together* (action), *say together* (language), and *stay together* (calm).

These four connection methods can be layered into a short ritual (perhaps two to five minutes) that can be used consistently during challenging transitions or when things go awry. This ritual can help meet a child's need for *always* and their need for a caring adult to help bring them back to center. CALM rituals allow caregivers to provide a sense of structure and of *always* even in moments when things feel unpredictable.

For some readers, the prospect of following this four-step recipe might feel overwhelming. *I'm supposed to do all those things when the child I care for is having a hard time?* The answer is both yes and no. While following these steps sequentially can be helpful, they don't require you to do anything new or add anything to your life. Instead, this recipe works best when you use the connection methods the child you care for already loves. It's also likely you're already doing some version of this during times of stress—we can think of CALM rituals as "emergency routines" that help us soothe or even prevent incidents of "emergency brain." Here's how the individual steps of a CALM ritual can help us keep our heads in tough moments—and help the kids we love feel more tranquil and balanced.

1. Be together

As we learned in the last chapter, the simple fact of our presence can be incredibly soothing to the kids we care for. While many preschoolers will feel comforted by

touch in challenging moments—a hug, a hand to hold—
others will prefer just to have a caregiver nearby, quietly
waiting for the storm to pass. By starting with closeness
in whatever form the child prefers, we acknowledge
that this is a moment in which they are in need of care
and steadying.

2. Do together

Synchronous movement can be just as soothing for
preschoolers as it is for younger children, but it may
take a different form than it once did. Some kids prefer
physically transitioning from one activity to another in
a playful way (jumping from one room to another like
a rabbit, for instance, or dancing over to the trash can
to help clean up), while others like the more tranquil
and traditional rocking. No matter what it looks like,
moving through transitions with a caregiver can reassure a preschooler that they're not alone.

3. Say together

Many preschoolers will have a favorite song or poem
that feels particularly soothing to them, that helps to

lighten their mood, or that helps to introduce and soften a transition to another activity. These "magic words" can be anything from a lullaby to a cartoon theme song to a hopscotch rhyme to a hymn. As it was in babyhood, combining the recitation of a preferred rhyme with other connection methods—particularly movement—can be incredibly soothing.

My personal favorite thing about magic words is their versatility. Depending on the needs of the child you care for, a song or poem can be used to introduce a new activity (like the "clean-up song" used in many preschool classrooms) or to help a child feel calm during a tense moment. No matter how it's used, it echoes the parentese so many children were exposed to in babyhood and reinforces the practice of consistency in a loving, soothing way.

4. Stay together

Babies are naturally inclined to mindfulness, and they call it forth in us. Many preschoolers will similarly call us to mindfulness by resisting transitions that feel rushed. Even when they seem to be recovering from a tantrum and returning to a place of calm and balance, a preschooler may still need a few moments with us before they can consider moving on to the next activity. By acknowledging their need to linger with us in the present moment, we show them that we understand their needs and seek to prioritize them.

THE WAY TO CONSISTENCY

Two Ways You Might Already Be Engaged in This Spiritual Practice

1. **Attuning to the elements**

   Nearly all of us are attuned to the connection methods the children we care for prefer, and we naturally use them to provide the soothing they require from time to time. If you find yourself taking note of the connection methods the preschooler in your care likes best (dancing together rather than rocking; singing this song rather than that one), you're improving your ability to comfort them.

2. **Using the elements individually and regularly**
   While some caregivers will naturally layer the elements of CALM into a longer ritual, others will find that using them individually, as needed, works better for the child in their care. To always sing a favorite song when a child is in need of soothing or always use a particular activity to introduce a hard transition is still to practice consistency and still to comfort a child in need. You can always layer them into a ritual later, if it makes sense to do so, but even using one at a time is helpful to the child you love!

Coming Up Next

In the next chapter, we'll be examining how the practice of peace can help you create a sense of tranquility for the preschoolers you care for. Before we move on, please take a moment to answer the questions here in whatever way works for you.

Reflection Questions

1. What sorts of connection methods do the preschoolers you care for seem to prefer? Are there specific words or actions that they seem to find especially soothing and regulating? Take a moment to brainstorm a few.

2. What elements of CALM do you find yourself already using when the preschoolers you care for are in need of comfort?

3. Do you notice particular times of day when the children you care for are consistently in need of calming? What connection methods could you use to make a CALM ritual that might make that time of day easier?

Chapter Nine

Peace

Input

Over my twenty years of working with preschoolers, many of the kids I cared for developed temporary fears of or aversions to sensory input. Many common sights, sounds, and smells—fluorescent lights buzzing overhead, the sound of traffic passing on the street—can trigger the kind of behavior that so many caregivers find challenging to handle. Even a seemingly simple after-school errand can become a minefield of over-stimulation. Take this example from a *Childcare*

Quarterly article by Louise Parks about teacher Amanda's trip to the grocery store with her preschool-age daughter in tow:

> She leaves work at 5 p.m. with her 4-year-old daughter and hits bumper-to-bumper traffic for the 20-minute drive to the grocery. The first stop at the grocery is the Ladies Room where Amanda and her daughter are blasted with the odor of room deodorizer, an auto-flushing toilet, store flyers posted on every wall, an electric hand dryer, and ringing cell phones in every stall. Then they head to the grocery aisles.

Amanda and her child are bombarded with an overwhelming number of noises, scents, and visuals even before their grocery shopping has really begun. Parks doesn't say how they react, but readers who have found themselves in a similar situation will find it easy to imagine Amanda clinging to her last shreds of patience as she steers her grocery cart down the crowded aisles in search of dinner while her hungry, tired, overstimulated four-year-old makes clear in every way available to her that this state of affairs is absolutely intolerable.

What do we caregivers do when the kids we love find the activities of everyday life frightening or overwhelming? What do we do when stores, toilets, and traffic provoke episodes of the "emergency brain" we explored in the last chapter? Many people feel out of their depth when trying to handle situations like these. Luckily, whether you know it or not, you're already in possession of a spiritual tool that can help everyone keep their composure: yourself.

Intentional Tranquility

As caregivers of young children, we already know that we're a safe place for the kids we love. As they grow and begin to explore the world around them, they'll come to us again and again for everything from comfort and consolation to encouragement and praise. Whether we know it or not, many of them return to us for something else as well: a brief respite from the noise, light, and general chaos of the modern world.

In an *Atlantic* article titled "The End of Silence," Bianca Bosker writes that over the past three hundred years "our soundscape has been overpowered by the steady roar of machines: a chorus of cars, planes, trains, pumps, drills, stereos, and turbines; of jackhammers, power saws, chain saws, cellphones, and car alarms, plus generators, ventilators, compressors, street sweepers, helicopters, mowers," and more. For children born in industrialized nations in the twenty-first century, these noises are everywhere, even in spaces designed for kids themselves. Studies from Sweden have found that the noise levels in preschool classrooms frequently approach (and sometimes exceed) those considered safe for human hearing. While the impact of this sort of sensory overstimulation on babies and young kids isn't yet fully understood, research detailed by Ron Chepesiuk in a paper evocatively called "Decibel Hell" has found that adults living in loud environments frequently display stress responses, depression, and anxiety. Fortunately, the children in our care will not necessarily suffer the same effects from noise. Since long before the invention of electric lights and combustion engines, adult caregivers have engaged in a spiritual practice that I believe is naturally protective against stress: the practice of peace.

I define the practice of peace as *the intentional creation of tranquility for those we love.* If you've cared for young children for any length of time—even one day!— you've likely practiced peace with them in ways that felt so natural that you didn't even realize you were doing it. Like the other practices discussed in this book, the practice of peace begins in babyhood and continues during the preschool years, taking new forms as the kids we love begin to request intermittent relief from the sensory input they receive from the world around them.

I believe that the practice of peace appears in two places that are hidden in plain sight: in the environment, and in our relationships.

Where Peace Appears

In the environment

Have you ever turned down the lights or closed the window shades to signal to a baby that it's time to sleep? Have you put on music or the fuzzy auditory blanket known as "white noise" to help soothe them? If so, you've modified a child's immediate environment to create periods of what's known as *sensory rest*, which Shauna Dalton-Smith, MD, defines in her book *Sacred Rest* as "the opportunity to downgrade the endless onslaught of . . . input received from electronics, fragrances, and background noise."

We may not really be aware of this onslaught until we find ourselves caring for an infant. I was a brand-new parent trying to coax my newborn to sleep before I noticed exactly how many barking dogs lived on my street or that my neighbor liked to use their leafblower every afternoon. Merely being in the presence of a baby immediately shifted my perception when it came to sensory input. *Was it always this loud?* The answer, of course, was yes, but I'd been so absorbed in other things that I hadn't tuned into it. Once I did, I found myself doing what many caregivers do: instinctively taking steps to insulate my child from excess sensory input and soothe her. When we do this, we unintentionally mimic the more subdued environment they knew before they were born, giving them the opportunity to reclaim, just for a moment, the greater serenity of that place.

In our relationships

While my definition of the practice of peace involves the intentional creation of tranquility, I don't believe it begins intentionally. Instead, like so many of the other practices we're examining in this book, it starts instinctively—baked into our relationships with children though the ways we care for them from the very start of life. Whether through cuddling, singing, or rocking (all behaviors that we know tend to come naturally to adults who are caring for infants), we gently stimulate a child's senses in ways that create quiet: not an absence of noise, but a sense of calm and stillness. This more spiritual quiet, child development researchers Jonathan R. Weber and Erica E. Ryherd have found, is highly protective against the effects of stress, overwhelm, and even physical pain.

For these reasons and more, it could be said that we don't practice peace *with* infants as much as we embody peace *for* them. We become it, using every-thing from the scent of our skin to the warmth of our voices to communicate our availability as calm, safe places. For years into the future, the children we love will associate us and our bodies with feelings of com-fort and serenity and will call on us to offer them this peace again and again.

Leaders of Peace

It's no surprise that many preschoolers will continue to associate our caring behaviors with feelings of com-fort and tranquility, or that many of them will prompt us to take the practice of peace from unconscious to purposeful through their more forthright requests for periods of sensory rest. What might come as a surprise is how these prompts will serve to shape us into the guides they need.

Studies of children's behavior in loud or chaotic environments have found that preschool-age kids move away from more passive coping behaviors they showed in babyhood. In a 2019 paper by Kerstin Persson Waye and others examining classroom noise from preschool teachers' perspective, teachers found that preschoolers move toward "actively seeking help and avoidance of sources of stress." In other words, **during the tending years preschoolers will look to loving adults to act as leaders of peace, asking to be guided day by day as they learn how to find relief from the tumult of the world.** As leaders of peace, we will step up to provide them this relief.

There are myriad ways a preschooler might ask us to provide this protection, but Persson Waye's research shows that two—one physical and one emotional—are most common. Let's consider them one at a time to discover how responding to these requests shifts our perspective and stretches us into the caregivers kids need.

Physical coping: blocking

In the study from Sweden referenced at the beginning of this chapter, four- and five-year-olds were found to develop coping mechanisms to deal with distressing or unpleasant noises in their environment and to request relief from nearby adults. (Although younger children weren't included in the study, anyone who's spent time with two- or three-year-olds knows that they too may develop strategies to limit sensory input and to request assistance.) The most common method of coping was to physically block out overwhelming levels of sensory input by covering the ears or attempting to hide. In addition to functioning as a coping mechanism, I believe that these behaviors can also be understood as a request for a caregiver to assist the child in limiting input from the environment the way we instinctively did for them when they were a baby.

In the short term, practicing peace by attending to and responding to these requests to change the environment helps bring a child relief. In the long term, I also think it helps remind us how little preschoolers still are. Although they often seem so big and capable compared to their infant selves, some preschoolers may have nearly as much trouble soothing themselves as they did when they were babies and will often request help in ways that seem immature. When they communicate their discomfort in ways that appear "babyish," we may be cued to nurture them with extra compassion and grace, similar to the way we instinctively engage with infants.

Emotional coping: not settling

Some caregivers may find that a child they care for is routinely restless or hyper at bedtime instead of sleepy. For some preschoolers, this behavior may be the result of an overabundance of sensory input over the course of the day. For these kids, the effects of sensory input are cumulative, meaning that they add up slowly to the point of overstimulation, which they reach just as we expect the child to go to sleep. I interpret the behavior we might notice in this situation—running around giggling instead of getting into pajamas; jumping on the bed instead of snuggling down into it—as a plea for relief from the stimulation of the day, which may have been invisible to us but overwhelming for the child. Translated, I imagine these actions to mean

> Preschool was fun but the room was so loud! Then we went to the park and there were so many dogs barking, then we got on the subway with all those people and got off at the doctor's office for my appointment—it's bright and it smells funny there and we saw a lot of people I didn't know. Then we went home (the subway was more crowded than before) and I watched TV for a while and then we had new food for me to try at dinner and now I'm too wired to sleep. Help!

The sensory input a child receives over the course of a day may be both varied and intense and comes from sources that are such a normal part of twenty-first-century life (a classroom, the park, the subway, the television, new food) as to be invisible to us. While a child may seem to cope well with each one over the course of the day, by the time evening comes they may have trouble settling as they struggle to "come down" from all the stimulation they've absorbed.

Over time, I believe attuning to this more subtle request for help can help us experience the world as the child we care for does: to be aware of the ways in which they are different from us, to notice what affects them, and to use this information to help. This increased empathy for their experience may allow us to respond compassionately to their needs even when we're tired, stressed, or overwhelmed ourselves.

THE WAY TO PEACE

Two Ways You Might Already Be Engaged in This Spiritual Practice

1. Limiting input as needed

In the same way we intuitively embody peace for infants, caregivers will often instinctively limit sensory input for preschoolers. We might avoid errands at certain times of day if the child we care for seems overwhelmed by them; we might limit screen time or music if we notice they over-stimulate instead of calm. These might seem like small interventions, but they can have a huge effect on a child's comfort level as they navigate the world with us.

2. **Planning ahead**

   One way caregivers might intentionally meet a child's need for sensory rest and protection is to plan ahead of time to practice peace with them when they need it. Over time, as we become increasingly attuned to what a preschooler's behavior might be requesting from us, we may notice particular days and times that they seem especially in need of sensory rest: after daycare, before bed, etc. When we make a plan to meet this need for tranquility—to turn down the lights, to put on soft music, or to use a CALM ritual filled with connection elements that work to soothe the child we love—we can feel more con-fident in our ability to act as leaders of peace.

Reflection Questions

1. In what ways do you find yourself practicing peace with the children you care for?

2. How do you notice the preschoolers you care for telling you they're in need of sensory rest?

3. Are there any times of day that you notice the preschoolers you care for seem especially in need of sensory rest? How might you be able to meet their need for increased peace?

Conclusion

I felt the urge to begin writing this book when my daughter was three. Now, as I finish it, she's weeks away from her tenth birthday. Life with a tween has few similarities to life with a preschooler and yet, as I reread what I have written here, I see how many things remain the same: it is still my calling as a caregiver to nourish, protect, and delight in my child. Restorative rituals at mealtimes, play times, and rest times still serve to connect us just as they did when she was small, even as they look profoundly different (and much more flexible) than they once did. We continue to grow together—her into her flourishing self, my wife and me into the parents she needs us to be. While our time in the tending years may have passed, much of what we did and learned together during that time lives on.

If you are reading this in the midst of your own tending years, I hope you take away the message that the simple, everyday ways you connect with the preschooler you care for are meaningful and incredibly special to them, even if they can't always show it in ways that are easy for adults to understand. If the kids you care for are stretching you to your limits of patience and stamina, I hope you know how much you're doing exactly right—because you are doing *so much* right!—and that there will be better, easier days to come.

I leave you with a blessing in solidarity with all caregivers that I wrote years ago, after a hard parenting day. I hope it helps you see, on your own hard days, how generous, helpful, loving, and wonder-filled you are. You are exactly the person the children you care for need, and I am grateful for you.

Litany of Thanks
For the Caregivers

Today, we were generous. That we had enough of ourselves to give, let us be thankful.

Today, we offered help. That our spirits are vibrant and our minds ready with solutions, let us be thankful.

Today, we loved another. That even now, in the midst of so many challenges, our hearts remain open, let us be thankful.

Today, we felt moments of joy and wonder. That joy and wonder remain so persistent—that they continue

163

to shimmer in the corners of our lives, in this broken world—let us be thankful.

For all that we have shared today, all that has passed between us and those we hold dear, let us give thanks.

Acknowledgments

I am deeply grateful to everyone who offered me love, support, and help while I was writing this book.

Mary Benard, Larisa Hohenboken, Pierce Alquist, and everyone at Skinner House Books were so incredibly generous during the writing and editing process. I couldn't be more thankful for the help and guidance I received from you all.

Christine Bulman and Jennifer Graham offered their expertise as early childhood educators to make this book a better one. Thank you so much for your kindness and your excellent editorial suggestions.

Colleen and George Anderson provided childcare so that I could have the time and space to write. Thank you for the love and care you offered (and the many games of Uno you played) so that this book had a chance to exist.

Teegan Dykeman-Brown, Monica Jacobson-Tennessen, Alix Klingenberg, Dawn MacKechnie, Samantha Myers, Ruth Owen, Sarah Smee, and Emily White gave ongoing moral support and spiritual nourishment as I wrote. Thank you for believing in me, for cheering me on, and for discussing the minutiae of the book publishing process for far longer than any human should be forced to tolerate.

The YADUUDes and craft night crew, including Shandi Bell, Kate Chase, Jennifer Lapointe, Brenton MacKechnie, Missy Schortmann, Amanda Singrassia and Heather Singrassia, have shared years of support and laughter. I am so lucky to have you all in my life!

Ceilidh MacKechnie, Tristan MacKechnie, and Roo Shattuck inspired this book by being the most delightful preschoolers ever to exist. Knowing you, and watching you grow into the lovely humans that you are has been a privilege and a joy. Thank you for being.

ACKNOWLEDGMENTS

Audra Shattuck, best of wives and best of women, was with me every step of the way. Thanks are not enough for all the love, comfort, sustenance, courage, and joy you have given me over the last twenty years. With you, everything is possible.

Suggested Reading

No Bad Kids: Toddler Discipline Without Shame by Janet Lansbury

Everyday Blessings: The Inner Work of Mindful Parenting by Myla and Jon Kabat-Zinn

How Toddlers Thrive: What Parents Can Do Today for Children Ages 2–5 to Plant the Seeds of Lifelong Success by Tovah P. Klein, PhD

Rest, Play, Grow: Making Sense of Preschoolers (Or Anyone Who Acts Like One) by Deborah MacNamara, PhD

Discovering The Culture of Childhood by Emily Plank